Learning through Dialogue

The Relevance of Martin Buber's Classroom

Kenneth Paul Kramer

ROWMAN & LITTLEFIELD EDUCATION
A division of
ROWMAN & LITTLEFIELD PUBLISHERS, INC.
Lanham • New York • Toronto • Plymouth, UK

Published by Rowman & Littlefield Education
A division of Rowman & Littlefield Publishers, Inc.
A wholly owned subsidiary of The Rowman & Littlefield Publishing Group, Inc.
4501 Forbes Boulevard, Suite 200, Lanham, Maryland 20706
www.rowman.com

10 Thornbury Road, Plymouth PL6 7PP, United Kingdom

British Library Cataloguing in Publication Information Available

Library of Congress Cataloging-in-Publication Data

Kramer, Kenneth Paul, 1941–
Learning through dialogue : the relevance of Martin Buber's classroom / Kenneth Paul Kramer.
pages cm
Includes bibliographical references and index.
ISBN 978-1-4758-0438-6 (cloth : alk. paper)—ISBN 978-1-4758-0439-3 (pbk. : alk. paper)—ISBN
978-1-4758-0440-9 (ebook)
1. Education—Philosophy. 2. Interaction analysis in education. 3. Dialogue analysis. 4. Buber, Martin, 1878-1965. I. Title.
LB775.B7493K73 2013
370.1—dc23
2013001185

™ The paper used in this publication meets the minimum requirements of
American National Standard for Information Sciences Permanence of Paper for Printed
Library Materials, ANSI/NISO Z39.48-1992.

Printed in the United States of America

Authentic education does not happen "on the broad upland of a system that includes a series of sure statements about the absolute, but a narrow rocky ridge between the gulfs where there is no sureness of expressible knowledge but the certainty of meeting what remains undisclosed."

—Martin Buber

For Maurice Friedman
Esteemed teacher, mentor, friend
Who "dared, despite all, to trust."

Contents

Foreword

Maurice Friedman

The "narrow ridge" is a phrase that was very important to Martin Buber. The "narrow ridge" means the unity of contraries, holding the tension between them instead of putting them into an either/or, which is our usual way of thinking. Martin Buber owes this idea originally to Nicholas of Cusa, a seventeenth-century theologian, who spoke of the coincidentia oppositorum. Kenneth Kramer has used this phrase in a highly meaningful and relevant way in Learning Through Dialogue. No one else, to my knowledge, has ever expanded upon Buber's metaphor so fully.

With a profound understanding of Buber's philosophy of dialogue and closely knit reasoning, Kenneth Kramer has made a convincing case for dialogue as the broadest educational frame, the methodology that goes beyond ordinary methodology. His ideas should be read slowly and thoughtfully.

I have written forewords for two other Kramer books that grew out of his present, whole-hearted allegiance to the thought of Martin Buber. Learning Through Dialogue, however, goes beyond these two, not only in its autobiographical accounts, but also in the carefully studied chapters on "inclusion," dialogue between teacher and student, dialogue with texts, interview dialogues, and journal dialogues. In my half-century of teaching in colleges and universities, I have approached education as dialogue through always having small classes in which there could be real mutuality and reciprocal respect. Kenneth Kramer has gone beyond that by finding new ways in which his students can fully participate in the learning community.

Martin Buber sees the central role of the teacher as drawing forth the student so that one reaches the student's speaking voice. In this process of drawing forth, the two-sided I-Thou relationship between teacher and student itself educates. Kramer suggests that "in order to enter into a genuine relaᴜᴜnship with another, one needs to overcome the way that one has been educated," that is, hearing only the teacher's voice, and seeing things only from the teacher's point of view. "Most of our encounters are lifted from their original dialogical voice and placed upon the pedestal of objective discourse." In his thirty years of university teaching and still today, Kramer cares deeply for the student as an equal partner in the teacher-student relationship.

Uniquely, Kramer devotes an entire chapter to Buber's concept of "inclusion," which Kalman Yoran, director of the Martin Buber Center of Adult Education, has called "Martin Buber's most original and significant contribution" to educational theory. "The teacher comes in person," writes Kramer, "to meet and to draw forth the student in new ways." Kramer continues, "Experiencing the student from the student's side of the relationship means in turn realizing the student's actual uniqueness and viewing the other person as fully meaningful." This type of inclusion, for Buber, is at the core of the teacher-student relationship. Inclusion—which literally means wrapping around and embracing—involves experiencing through the student's eyes and ears. Boldly swinging to the student's side is accompanied almost simultaneously by bringing back to one's own side as much of the student's own situation as one can glean.

Kramer makes a brilliant connection between Buber's "unteaching" and the Taoist *wu-wei*—doing as though you are not doing—harkening back to Buber's early interest in Taoism. To illustrate what he means about teaching as though you are not teaching, Martin Buber used "the funnel" and "the pump" to describe two different approaches to education, which we might call the "conservative" or traditional approach and the "progressive" approach. The "funnel" suggests that a student's mind is an open receptacle into which the teacher pours his or her knowledge. The "pump" implies a confidence in the student as the source of true education as it manifests itself. Here, dialogue is a third alternative to the funnel and the pump: dialogue used, as Martin Buber used the word, to describe a wholehearted reciprocal turning to the other. This, I think, is the meaning of learning through dialogue.

My delight intensified when I read the account that Kramer gave of Buber's approach to education in practice—an account that gives a special flavor to this rare and unusual book on teaching and learning. Kramer includes interviews with three experts on the interrelationship between dying and dialogue. He connected his work with that of a number of other experts on dying and the centers in which they worked in California. These interviews make excellent reading.

His particular interest is the field of religious studies, which he rightly says involves many different methodologies that need to be used and, if possible, brought into dialogue with one another. Kramer carries this thinking over into the differences between one person and another. Instead of agreement, harmony, and certainty, dialogians are more concerned with depth of listening, accuracy of expression, and clarity of understanding. Kramer speaks about the unfortunate flight from dialogue that he recognizes in so much contemporary writing.

I am ninety years old. In the last sixty years I have not read any book that has the depth, perspicacity, insight, and personal honesty of Kramer's Learning Through Dialogue. It has been a blessing for me to have a friend and colleague such as Kenneth Kramer.

Maurice Friedman
Professor Emeritus of Religious Studies, Philosophy,
and Comparative Literature
San Diego State University

Preface

Don't forget: everybody must give something back for something they get . . .

—Bob Dylan, "Fourth Time Around"

How do you respond to one of the single most important questions asked of teachers: Not what, but *how* do you teach? What critical powers and habits of mind and spirit do you practice in the classroom and encourage your students to exercise? What keeps you passionate about the craft of teaching?

Pedagogical self-reflection is not a matter of idle speculation. It is central to our practice as teachers and students. It is not, however, an area to which many of us devote sufficient attention. This book teaches us how practicing Martin Buber's dialogical principles uniquely addresses these questions.

GENESIS

One sunny, early fall afternoon, I began thinking of my thirty years of university teaching. I was daydreaming, really, about how academic studies could be advanced. How could theories and methods be rethought in a way that would liberate both the teaching and the studying of human experience? Indeed, how should the word *teaching* be thought of?

I was sitting at my large desk staring out through the picture window opening onto the garden. Classical music played in the background. It was shortly after 2 p.m., a little over half an hour before my daily 3 o'clock infusion of fresh fruit and organic java with honey and a splash of half-and-half. At that moment, before I could account for it, the next thing I knew I was on the other side of an explosion. Before I realized its full force, a confluence of refracted insights coalesced around the word *pedagogy*.

What happened? A "call" presented itself in the depths of my being. It wasn't like Isaiah or Jeremiah's prophetic calls. They saw visions, heard voices, were touched on the lips by the celestial messenger, and were commissioned to speak in the name of the Lord.

Rather, I was filled with a realization, a deep awareness that seemed to be rising from the created world and presenting itself to me. This explosion, hitting me with the force of a powerful energy, opened a door directly into vivid memories of my years in the classroom.

"Of course!" I realized. "If I know about anything well, it's about university teaching." In that moment, a sequence of quickly appearing-and-disappearing images, ideas, memories, and insights flashed in my consciousness: Bob Dylan lyrics; previous publications; teaching experiences; the current state of undergraduate instruction; forthcoming lectures; Martin Buber's dialogical pedagogy; conversations with my mentor and Buber scholar, Maurice Friedman. The raw material for this little book was already taking shape.

TEACHER, TAUGHT, AND TEACHING

But why is this book important? I'll let two eminent educators, who have deeply influenced me, speak to this question. First, Confucius. He collected, internalized, and taught humanistic attitudes and, in the process, developed a pedagogy of clarifying concepts and names and thereby reanimating tradition. For Confucius: "To learn and at due times to repeat what one has learned, is that not after all a great pleasure?" He followed this with: "He who by reanimating the Old can gain knowledge of the New is fit to be a teacher."[1]

Confucius's genius was to selectively preserve the classics, to transmit them with reanimated meaning, and thereby to restore an ancient harmony between the teacher, the taught, and the teaching.

Second, Martin Buber. One of Buber's major contributions to the educational process was his introduction of the teacher's main tool—dialogue. Like Confucius's pedagogy of reanimation, Buber's educational approach is shaped by reciprocal interactions between and among teacher, taught, and teaching. That Buber's dialogical pedagogy is honest, exact, original, even life-impacting seems obvious. But this book touches upon something less obvious: real teachers, Buber tells us, participate in "the secret history of the world."[2]

The first thing one realizes about Buber's philosophy of education is how radically perceptive it is. It can be summed up in two words: "relationship educates."[3] Buber indicates that almost nothing is more important, more revitalizing than the education of character. And here's his major breakthrough: real learning happens neither because of the teacher's brilliant artic-

ulations nor the student's fidelity to the task, but the reciprocal be
the two.

Though central to his own life, this practical concept is often ~
or undervalued by Buber scholars and general readers alike. When was the
last time—if ever—that you heard of the educational implications of Buber's
philosophy? Who speaks persuasively of an educational praxis of dialogue?
In this book, we will explore how Buber's educative model "provides us with
some possible curricular and pedagogical approaches which allow us to enable learners—both 'teachers' and 'students'— . . . to embody dialogue in an
integrated and reflective fashion."[4]

PROFESSOR AND STUDENT

Throughout these chapters, to concretely illustrate significant points, I inter-
sperse references to the educational impact of two relationships central to my
own life, one with Professor Maurice Friedman (1921–2012), the world's
leading authority on Martin Buber and my dissertation advisor,[5] and the
other with Todd Perreira, one of my best students at San José State University.

It was through the PhD program in religion and literature that Friedman
founded and directed at Temple University in the late 1960s and early 1970s,
and through the influence of his book *To Deny Our Nothingness*, that I first
came to meet Maurice Friedman. One of my earliest significant memories of
him was learning in his seminars to avoid the temptation to reduce literature
to "contents" or "themes" or "symbols," and to develop a dialogical approach
to human experience.

The other was the way he illustrated Buber's back-and-forth movement
between "I-Thou" experiential encounters and "I-It" representations of
events. Extending his right hand, fingers down, he would trace an invisible
infinity sign with his hand, his fingers turning upside down as they traced
their way back up the curve and then turning facedown upon reaching the top
of the other curve. Buber's words, along with Friedman's clarifications and
applications, have become powerfully life-changing.

It was in my Death, Dying, and Religions class at San José State University that I first met Todd Perreira. My earliest memory of Todd was his
extraordinary thoroughness and remarkable competence in completing class
work. He was one of the few students I've taught who actually wanted to
read more than what was assigned. His enthusiasm for learning initiated a
relationship in which he took all of my classes. When he graduated from San
José State, he went on to receive a master's degree at Harvard University
Divinity School and a PhD at the University of California at Santa Barbara.

Since his return to San José State as a lecturer, he has invited me to speak about Martin Buber's dialogical philosophy in one of his classes every semester. It is almost as if I could say of him, as he once said of me, that he demonstrates the relationship between the practical and the theoretical by espousing the dialogical approach, showing again and again that genuine relationship is "immensely difficult yet totally accessible with trust or what Maurice Friedman . . . calls existential grace."[6] My dialogues with Friedman and with Perreira continue to address and enrich my life.

VISION

Looking back on my thirty years of teaching, I realize that the communication between teachers and students is often inadequate and one-sided. Because the level of communication is not communicative in its own right, educational content doesn't stick and students aren't engaged. In our digital culture, real educational communication is a rarity.

The solution, I believe, lies in Buber's principles of genuine dialogue, which reshape the traditional power dynamic between teacher and student. Why? Because genuine dialogue, according to Buber, has three voices— yours, mine, and the voice of the dialogical relationship itself.

This book offers an alternative approach to teaching and learning, in the humanities and social sciences, that utilizes Buber's dialogical principles of *turning toward*, *addressing affirmatively*, *listening attentively*, and *responding responsibly*. The end goal is for teachers and students alike to engage each other and the material studied in ways that challenge self-concepts and call for a new relational thinking. For Buber, the objective of education is the transformation of the ways in which people interact with each other.

Learning Through Dialogue does not attempt to make a full-on academic appraisal of the teaching-learning process. These chapters are academic enough to serve as a valuable text for university teachers and students preparing to teach, yet interpersonal enough to be read for pleasure as well as profit by those no longer in school.

If you are a teacher, student, an educator of educators (university, community college, high school), a school administrator, counselor, curriculum specialist, school board member, parent, or anyone interested in furthering his or her ability to engage more meaningfully with education itself, this book will challenge you with its fresh perspective.

The focus of this book is on what teachers and educators should know about Buber, the relevance and meaning of his theory, and how his methods can be implemented in daily classroom instruction. My earnest hope is that you may say, in reading this book, "I wish I would have had a teacher who taught me like this," just as I have said, many times in my career, "I wish I could be a teacher more like this."

NOTES

1. *The Analects of Confucius*, trans. Arthur Waley (New York: Vintage Books, 1938), I, 1; II, 11.

2. Martin Buber, *Mamre: Essays in Religion*, trans. Greta Hort (Westport, Conn.: Greenwood Press, 1946), 63.

3. Martin Buber, *A Believing Humanism*, trans. Maurice Friedman (New York: Simon and Schuster, 1967), 98. Buber writes that what he means by educating is no "content of an utterance, but the speaking voice; no instructing, but the glance, the movement, the being-there of those teaching when they are inspired by the educational task. Relationship educates . . . provided that it is a genuine educational relationship."

4. Charles Scott, in his dissertation *Becoming Dialogue; Martin Buber's Concept of Turning to the Other as Educational Praxis*, Simon Fraser University, 2011.

5. Buber died in 1965, leaving behind a vast library of his writings along with numerous students and scholars eager to engage with his thought. Maurice Freidman, who died just before this book went to press, is/was one of the most prominent scholars. Buber and Freidman shared a professional as well as personal relationship, which is reported in Maurice Freidman's *My Friendship With Martin Buber* (New York: Syracuse University Press, 2013).

6. Todd Perreira, January 25, 1995, letter to the Outstanding Professor Committee at San José State University.

Acknowledgments

I owe an enormous amount to many people and recognize that this book is made possible by the courageous and creative interactions, relationships, and actions that these people have taken. With a profound gratitude, I especially acknowledge:

Maurice Friedman, my dissertation advisor at Temple University (1968–1971), introduced me in his teaching and writings to the life-transformative significance of Martin Buber's philosophy of dialogue and the pedagogical power of Buber's educational theory, and encouraged me to complete this book.

Those teachers, both undergraduate and graduate, who captivated my attention and interest through their words, gestures, style, and especially by the quality of their questions, which impacted my life in ways that allowed me to enrich the lives of my students as well.

Dan Shea, a fellow graduate student at Temple University, opened up profound insights into the educational process, some of which carried forward into this book. When I quoted Ezra Pound's audacious *ABC of Reading* in the introduction, a book that we discussed to our mutual benefit, I knew that Dan's influence shone through some of my words.

My students at Saint Andrew's Presbyterian College (1967–1968), Temple University (1969–1970), LaSalle College (1971–1974), and especially San José (California) State University (1976–2001), whom I have had the privilege and responsibility to instruct and who, in the process, taught me.

My daughters, Leila Ann and Yvonne Rose, whom I raised as a single parent from the ages of eight and six, and who, to this day, challenge me to teach what is most important to me, to live what I teach, and to always, always be ready to hear what they have to say.

Sienna Rose, my granddaughter, who turned one just as I sent the manuscript for this book to the publisher. Our games of peek-a-boo never failed to get my creative energies flowing.

James Brown, my former student, who has gone on for a PhD in American studies and who read a version of this manuscript and made many extremely valuable suggestions that improved everything from sentence structure to narrative flow, including adding a sentence or two here and there to further clarify and solidify the text. He looked for and found what's new, what's fresh, what hadn't yet been noticed with skill and with creative attunement.

Pat Boni, a fellow student of Maurice Friedman and a former professor of religious studies at San Diego State University, read the manuscript closely, carefully, and creatively. With extraordinary skill, she caught and corrected mistakes, misstatements, and misspellings.

Jo Beck, my able typist, parachuted down to work with me from the beginning to near completion of the project's initial draft, including reading the manuscript for typos, formatting, tenses, and clarity of expression. And all this happened just before she completed her hundredth jump.

Lauren Greer, my closing typist, who will laughingly show her parents this acknowledgment. Lauren asked trajectory-altering questions and made multiple structure-enriching suggestions that are now, thankfully, embedded in the book. She introduced me to heretofore unknown, outside-of-my-comfort zone yet nevertheless appreciated cultural and Inter(net) connections.

Tom Koerner, the gatekeeper for this book's publication, posed personable questions, concerns, and reminders that were invaluable. In our ongoing dialogues about this project, he kept me focused on what teachers and educators should know about the relevance and meaning of Martin Buber's educational theory and methods and directed me to a wider audience than I had first imagined.

Introduction

Why is this book valuable? There exists a pervasive human relational problem in our culture, one shared by everyone, yet which drives a seemingly
impenetrable wedge between us all. That problem is the lack of real dialogue.
The term "dialogue," unfortunately, is understood by very few people who
actually use it. Some have even turned the word inside out, evoking the value
of dialogue while implementing a dual-monologue, no different than dialec-
tic or debate.

Assuming that there is only one right answer to a question derails the
educational process. Rather than encouraging a collaborative conversation,
monologue leads to miscommunication in which one enters the discussion
with a close-minded, even adversarial attitude. When one is close-minded or
adversarial, one listens to and addresses the other to prove him or her wrong.
It is through a dialogical exchange of ideas that real education occurs.

What is needed is a workable solution, a solution that truly considers
every person in their particular situation. This force, however, is not without
limits. During a dialogue with Professor Maurice Friedman at San José State
University, he once said:

> There are several limits [to dialogue]: one is time; one is hunger; and one is
> that you do what you can in a situation. There are even tragic situations where
> there are simply not enough resources on either side for a genuine meeting to
> take place. You don't insist on the dialogue and you don't assume it will
> always happen—you are simply open for it. If I could make dialogue happen,
> that wouldn't be dialogue. That would be willfulness. So I have my radius. I
> can prevent it, though. There can be a one-sided prevention of dialogue. I can
> do it simply by saying—"nothing's going to get through to me." But when
> there's a *willingness* for dialogue, then—and you used the word earlier—one
> must "navigate" moment-by-moment. It's a listening process.[1]

When asked "What advice would you give to other teachers?," Tim Gunn states, "Be a keen listener." If not, students will discredit you.[2]

WHY BUBER?

Martin Buber's own education was the product of two cultures, European (especially the German philosophical and literary traditions) and Jewish (especially Hebrew humanism). Gradually, these influences blended together and consequently emerged as his unique dialogical anthropology.

Buber's distinctive insights into the relationship between educational theory and what it means to be educated are essential to the structure of this book. Unfortunately many students of Martin Buber are unfamiliar with his work on education. This stems, in part, from the fact that Buber's writings on education are scattered throughout his other works.[3]

Martin Buber (1878–1965) was one of the greatest thinkers of the twentieth century. An internationally acclaimed philosopher, a consummate scholar, and a translator of the Hebrew Bible into German, Buber almost single-handedly introduced the communal Jewish mysticism of eighteenth-century Eastern Europe called Hasidism into Western civilization. His lyrical, philosophical classic, *I and Thou* (1923/1958)—translated into more than twenty languages—is universally recognized as one of the most influential books of the twentieth century.

The Russian literary and cultural theorist Mikhail Bakhtin called Buber "the greatest philosopher of the twentieth century."[4] In the words of Buber's friend Hermann Hesse, "Buber was one of the wisest persons living in the world."[5] Yet why is it important in the twenty-first century to study the dialogical philosophy of Martin Buber, who wrote in the last century? What can Buber show us, today, about our practice as teachers and learners?

Martin Buber's philosophy of genuine dialogue (spoken or silent) between persons is both the *foundation of* and *integral to* teaching and learning. "Martin Buber," as Buber's close friend Albrecht Goes writes, "is an educator by nature and by grace; he is possessed of the cardinal virtue of the educator—patience."[6]

In a similar vein, Aubrey Hodes, who befriended Buber toward the end of Buber's life, writes that he "was an educator, in the true sense of the word and in the limits of his own definition of it. He did not try to impose a self-evident formula upon his pupils, but posed questions which forced them to find their own answers. He did not want his pupils to follow him docilely but to take their own individual paths, even if this meant rebelling against him, because for him education meant freedom, a liberation of personality."[7]

Hodes exemplifies this in his comments by quoting what Buber once said to a group of twenty-five teachers who met at Buber's house to discuss problems facing Israeli teachers: "Everything depends on the teacher . . . as a person. He educates from himself, from his virtues and his faults, through personal example and according to circumstances and conditions. His task is to realize the truth in his personality and to convey this realization to the pupil."[8]

From Buber's perspective, the educational process involves more than analyzing, comparing, and evaluating various categories of thought. Instead, for Buber, knowledge is derived dialogically. His dialogical approach to knowing holds that through the immediacy of contact we come to more fully know a subject in its wholeness, in its uniqueness, and in its relationship to ourselves. Buber said, "I have no teaching, but I carry on a conversation."[9]

STRUCTURE

The problem with educational practice today is that it fails to make the crucial distinction between learning as an accumulation of information and learning as a dialogical interaction that elicits one's personal response to the material. This book offers both theoretical and practical material designed to incite classroom engagement with the material, with the teacher, and with each other as well as prompt further personal reflections.

Learning Through Dialogue is divided into two parts, each chapter concluding with points to remember. These chapters first present Buber's educational theory and method descriptively, then illustratively as they are practiced, especially in the humanities and social sciences.

In the second part of this book, specific examples are used to suggest some ways that Buber's philosophy of dialogue can be applied in the classroom. This part discusses the practical application of Buber's ideas to four different types of educational dialogues: (1) dialogues with a text as a Thou; (2) dialogues with students in class; (3) interview dialogues; and (4) journal dialogues.

Chapter 1 explores Buber's two ways of learning, dialogically and monologically. These two ways of communicating determine one's relation to the world and others, whether through two-sided I-Thou relationships or one-sided I-It relations. I-Thou relationships bring about real engagement in the classroom because they *include* three voices: the speaker's, the listener's, and the voice of the dialogue itself. Its four main elements include: turning, addressing, listening, and responding. In practicing genuine dialogue, one relearns his or her identity through reciprocity.

Chapter 2 shifts from Buber's bipolar educational theory to his method of inclusion, which embodies listening to the other (person/text) both from your side and by imaginatively experiencing the other's side. Inclusion is the practice of empathetically encountering the other person's thoughts, feelings, and experiences. One-sided inclusion occurs when only one person in the conversation is able to practice full mutuality. Practicing one-sided inclusion allows teachers to more engagingly and accurately communicate with students.

Chapter 3 depicts how teaching becomes unteaching when one is influenced and directed by the back-and-forth dynamic rhythm of intersubjectivity (which occurs on the "narrow ridge"). Unteaching refers to the practice of allowing the dialogue to teach both student and teacher; this process cannot be described as teacher-centered or student-centered, but as dialogue-centered. Teaching intersubjectively allows ideas to emerge from the exchange between and among teacher, students, and teaching. Ideally, the teacher addresses the whole student rather than the student as an object of the teacher's experience.

Chapter 4 looks at dialogue as a meta-methodology that integrates diverse, even conflicting, theories and methods through practicing openness to all voices. A learning community should embody diversity, ambiguity, creative conflict, honesty, humility, and freedom. However, this can only be achieved with a dialogical method that allows conflicting viewpoints to implicate—highlight and challenge—each other. This interhuman reality signifies a place (mutuality) and calls for an interaction (dialogue).

Chapter 5 focuses on ways of applying Buber's dialogical methodology to texts. In Buber's dialogical hermeneutics, a text speaks as a Thou and elicits awareness of the connection between that text and our own lives. Reading a text as a Thou challenges readers to engage it personally, as a voice that invites response, rather than as an It, as frozen words on a page. Engaging texts in this way requires: receptivity, suspension of bias, reflection, and application; by reacting to the voice of a text, the reader clarifies his or her stance.

Chapter 6 looks at various ways in which dialogue with students occurs and suggests strategies for creating a dialogical climate in the classroom. Unfortunately, when one cannot step outside of self-preoccupations, one misses another's invitation to engage in dialogue. Entering into genuine dialogue by turning away from the self and fully toward the other remedies this. A dialogical approach to education always opens up time for questions and discussion.

Chapter 7 introduces the interview dialogue as a specific type of conversation in which, after asking a knowledgeable person preplanned questions, the interviewer transitions into a spontaneous, unscripted exchange. Two essential elements of interview dialogues are discernment listening and interactive questioning. It is most important that the interviewee feels comfortable, feels important, and feels heard. Examples of this process occur in interviews with Elizabeth Kübler-Ross, Ram Dass, and Brother David Steindl-Rast.

Chapter 8 describes the practice of keeping dialogue journals—with others, with texts, with art, with the class—which provide occasions for deep reflection on *what* you are doing, *why* you are doing it, and *how* it can best be done. There are three forms of journal keeping: outer dialogues, inner dialogues, and feedback dialogues. The purpose of keeping a journal is to clarify the journal keeper's views, which then provides further opportunity to dialogue with others. The journal, for a teacher, allows him or her to make fresh connections with the course material and correspondingly recover the importance of students' views.

THE CHALLENGE

Why *Learning Through Dialogue* is organized this way is easy to explain. The two constitutive sides or elements of the educational process—theory/method and application/practice—are inseparable. Neither side of the teaching/learning coin can actively participate in the educational process without the other.

Each adds clarity to and exemplifies the other. Without theory and method, application/practice would lack justification and direction. Without application and practice, theory/method would lack corroboration from situations in which it has to authenticate itself. These two elements vividly demonstrate the need for intellectually enriching educational dialogues between teachers and students, and students, teachers, and the voice of the material studied.

The educational process is ignited by reciprocal dialogues. By distinguishing between the two main components of this book, readers will become more aware of the necessary connections between them. The question, which side is more important—theoretical ideas or practical enactments—resolves itself through the continued interplay of the book's two halves.

"Nobody knows everything about anything."[10] It is imperative, therefore, that one learns by actively engaging with educative materials, with teachers and students, and with one's own critical reflections, rather than just passively archiving data. It cannot be overemphasized that in order to find value in a classroom setting, we must develop the skill of talking with, not at, each other.

This approach allows teachers and students to expand their personal lenses. Rather than imposing his or her perspectives and values on students, the dialogical teacher encourages students to consider and allow course content to develop in ways that are uniquely appropriate. Students in turn grow through their encounter with the person of the teacher and the Thou of the writers studied—an encounter that transforms potential to actual, abstract to concrete, the unrelated to the immediate.

Successful teaching, therefore, involves mastery of a craft, and the craft of teaching involves the art of igniting the learning flame. One way to ignite this flame is through the practice of *teaching and learning as genuine dialogue*. Real education—not merely sheep-herding—arises and continues to fructify in the interaction between and among teacher, students, and subject matter studied.[11] Each has a voice, a stand, and a perspective that shapes and is reshaped by the other.

This practice involves building intergroup trust, developing instructional strategies that promote participation and learning in our classes, understanding and integrating methodological differences between the often-conflicting ideas we teach, and accommodating and encouraging diverse learning styles. Most importantly, real education involves authenticating the spirit of dialogue in our own classroom behaviors.

NOTES

1. Maurice Friedman, in *Dialogically Speaking: Maurice Friedman's Interdisciplinary Humanism*, ed. Kenneth Paul Kramer (Eugene, Ore.: Pickwick Publications, 2011), xxiii.

2. Stephen Vider, "You, Too, Can Make it Work," *New York Times, Education Life*, January 3, 2013, 29.

3. "Education" and "The Education of Character" in Martin Buber, *Between Man and Man*, trans. Ronald Gregor Smith (New York: The Macmillan Company, 1948); "Education and World-view" in Martin Buber, *Pointing the Way*, trans. Maurice Friedman (New York: Schocken Books, 1957); "Educating," "The Task," "On Contact," and "Style and Instruction" in Martin Buber, *A Believing Humanism: Gleanings*, trans. Maurice Friedman (New York: Simon and Schuster, 1969); "Teaching and Deed" and "On National Education" in Martin Buber, *Israel and the World, Essays in a Time of Crisis* (New York: Schocken Books, 1948).

4. See Maurice Friedman, "Martin Buber and Mikhail Bakhtin: The Dialogue of Voices and the Word That Is Spoken," *Religion and Literature* 33 (2001): 25–36.

5. Maurice Friedman, *Encounter on the Narrow Ridge: A Life of Martin Buber* (New York: Paragon House, 1991), ix.

6. Albrecht Goes, *Men of Dialogue: Martin Buber and Albrecht Goes*, ed. William Rollins and Harry Zohn (New York: Funk & Wagnalls, 1969), 197.

7. Aubrey Hodes, *Martin Buber: An Intimate Portrait* (New York: Viking Press, 1971), 118. Hodes remarks that Buber's "method was not pedagogical, in the narrow sense. He was little concerned with the how of teaching, with such matters as syllabuses, methods, and examinations. What concerned him was the why—how to give the pupil a sense of his identity, of his organic unity; how to show him the way to responsibility and love" (121).

8. Hodes, *Martin Buber*, 127.

9. Martin Buber, *The Philosophy of Martin Buber*, ed. Paul Arthur Schilpp and Maurice Friedman (La Salle, Ill.: Open Court, 1967), 693.

10. Leonard Swidler, "Humankind from the Age of Monologue to the Age of Global Dialogue," *Journal of Ecumenical Studies* 47, no. 3 (Summer 2012): 470.

11. I borrow the "sheep-herding" image from Ezra Pound, who says: "Real education must ultimately be limited to [people] who INSIST on knowing, the rest is mere sheep-herding." See *ABC of Reading* (New York: New Directions, 1960), 84.

Part I

Theory and Method

Chapter One

Buber's Two Ways of Learning

In a major collection of essays, Martin Buber asks, then answers, a question with which our exploration begins: Is there a central principle of education that can be considered a fixed maxim? Is there a universal norm that must be adhered to if the educational process is to be effective? Buber says: No, "what is called so was always only the norm of a culture, of a society, a church, an epoch."[1] The only thing that can be called a principle of education is the place where education begins—the starting point of teaching and learning. So where does Buber begin?

WHY DIALOGUE AROSE

The practice of educative dialogue is at least as old as ancient Greek culture. If we reflect on the term *dialogue*, we see that the Greek prefix *"dia"* has a variety of meanings, including: across, among, through, together. The Greek word *"logos"* has many cognates as well, including: reason, law, truth, Word. Thus etymologically, *"dia-logos"* means speaking meaningfully between people.

Socrates, for example, posed questions to his students and often responded by finding their answers untenable. Although Buber admired Socrates as one of the few people in history whom he both trusted and venerated, he did not accept the method of Socratic questioning. Buber said, "These are not real questions; they are moves in a sublime dialectical game that has a goal, the goal of revealing a not-knowing."[2] To discover the students' unique experiences, the teacher must ask real (i.e., situation-specific) questions, not just Socratic ones.

It makes sense in this context to ask about the rise of dialogue in the modern era. Along with the rapid development of communications, travel, and the world economy, our need to understand each other's perspectives has become more urgent. Even before entering into genuine dialogue, it is necessary to remember its contextual underpinnings:

- *Intention*—To understand what another person says, one needs to understand the intention of that person's statement;
- *Perspective*—Every statement is interpreted through the personal lens of the perceiver.

Martin Buber further developed these underpinnings by reintroducing dialogue—this time, as a lifestyle—into the West in his 1923 groundbreaking work, *I and Thou*. His thesis is: all real living, and by implication all real educating, flows from engaging and being engaged in genuine relationships. In *I and Thou*, Buber distinguished two basic orientations: one that prompts dialogue and the other that impedes it.

PRIMARY LIFE-STANDS

The opening sentence of *I and Thou* expresses a radical departure from several centuries of Western philosophical thought. To humans, Buber began, "the world is two-fold in accordance with his two-fold attitude."[3] This first sentence embodies one of Buber's most profound and far-reaching insights into human existence. These two modes of knowing, Buber explains, are related to the two basic ways that people communicate: I-Thou and I-It.[4] These are the two ways in which we relate to whomever and whatever we meet.

This lays the cornerstone of Buber's "life of dialogue." Buber clarifies that there are two ways of *standing* in the world, two ways in *communicating* with the world (translated in *I and Thou* as a twofold attitude) that flow through each person into the world of lived experiences. We can choose to relate to the world either as an It (an impersonal object of my experience) or as a Thou (a personal other who engages me).

I-Thou knowing is direct, intersubjective, dialogical, a knowing that cannot occur apart from interactive relationships and from which I-It knowledge is derived. By contrast, I-It knowledge is indirect, categorical, monological in that spoken words function as static entities. Each mode of knowledge plays an important role in one's total education.

Since Buber's educational theory is anchored in the opening sentence of *I and Thou*, let us consider more closely what he meant by twofold attitude (*Haltung*), by understanding I-Thou and I-It.[5] These word pairs are primary because they establish two fundamental ways of speaking in the world. "I" exists only in relation to the other, whether I relate to the other as a Thou or as an objectified It. Whenever we speak, we manifest the I, our chosen subject position, and take our stand therein.

In I-It relations—standing in proximity to the other—we remain outside our interactions by controlling the beginning, middle, and end; the subject discussed; and how it is defined. We see the other as an object of our experience, use that object for some purpose, and add the achievement of that purpose to the content of our knowing.

In I-Thou relationships—reciprocal engagements with another—we yield self-control naturally and spontaneously. We speak with our whole being and experience the dialogue as an event in our lives. Buber says: "When I confront a human being as my Thou and speak the basic word I-Thou . . . He is no longer He or She, limited by other Hes and Shes, a dot in the world grid of space and time, nor a condition that can be experienced and described, a loose bundle of named qualities."[6]

By "relation," Buber meant an association of proximity, merely occupying a similar place without necessarily becoming deeply connected. By "relationship," he was referring to a deep, bonding connection between one person and another. Relationship (*Beziehung*) describes a mutual presence, to a connection that embodies a past, a present, and a potential for the future. Relationship refers to a human bonding in which both partners affirm, accept, and confirm each other.

THE "THOU" WORLD AND EDUCATION

It is crucial to grasp the fact that when Buber speaks of the two primary word pairs, he means to indicate two fundamental ways of responding to, or communicating with, whatever is before us. When a person says I, she or he uses one of these two manners of speaking and no more. Thus, we continue to reposition ourselves relationally.

Neither exists in a pure state; they usually interact. The point, however, is this: in any given moment, one relates to the world *primarily* through one of these polarities. Because we make I-It primary in most of our interactions, we must not become stuck or trapped in I-It monologues. While our lives in the world benefit in practical ways because of I-It relations, developing personal wholeness requires I-Thou relationships.

One becomes fully human only in I-Thou relationships; only these types of relationships bring about a person's unique wholeness. Buber says, "I become I through my relation to the Thou; as I become *I*, I say *Thou*."[7] That is, one becomes genuinely human with and through the recognition of the dialogical Thou. Encounter—or relationship—is central to this experience. As Buber writes: "Primary words do not signify things, but they intimate

Table 1.1.

I-It Relations	I-Thou Relationships
Never Spoken with the Whole Being	Spoken with the Whole Being
Experiencing/Using/Knowing	Event/Happening
In Space and Time	Spaceless/Timeless
One-sided: Singular	Two-sided: Mutual
Controlling	Yielding
Subject-Object Duality	Interhuman Betweeness
Monologue	Dialogue

relation[ships]. Primary words do not describe something that might exist independent of them, but being spoken they bring about existence."[8]

In I-Thou relationships one engages the other (whether person, nature, text, or idea) personally and dialogically. Thus, I-Thou refers to a two-sided event in which uniqueness encounters uniqueness. When this occurs, dialogical understanding—as meaningful speech between one active existence and another—is reanimated.

THE "IT" WORLD AND EDUCATION

Buber never denied the value of the It world. He recognized the need for the conventional, objectivistic, and pragmatic. While I-It relations are not the end goal in a dialogical approach to education, they can lead toward an I-Thou relationship with the material. However significant I-It knowledge may be in regulating our daily lives, it is insufficient in addressing the wholeness and uniqueness of people or the materials.

The more we rely on rational discourse alone, on the necessary but insufficient world of I-It, the more we remove the educational process from our immediate, concrete situation, and the more we separate our students from each other and from ourselves.

All of our interactions occur between the It world and the Thou world. In everyday life, the two are often intertwined. Without realizing it, a Thou may become an It and an It may become a Thou. This switching between It and Thou can be instantaneous in some cases or gradual in others. We can switch from a concern with this object versus that object to a concern with entering into relationship and creating contexts for genuine educational dialogue.

What difference does it make whether we relate to the world of people, things, and events as Thous or as Its? What are the consequences of these different associations? In *Celebrating the Other*, Edward Samson suggests that a reorientation from monologue to dialogue could mark a revolutionary shift in Western intellectual history, in how we encounter the other. This applies in the humanities and social sciences as well as to society as a whole.

Monologism in these disciplines promotes the concept of the person as the self-contained individual. It demonstrates a teacher's failure to closely attend to speech of others, especially his or her students. Speaking monologically, both consciously and unconsciously, legitimizes the sole authority of the instructor.

Our propensity for a mono-language ignores the unique individuality of our students, and therefore rarely addresses the central pedagogical issues, which are larger than a single consciousness can perceive. To get at these issues, it is necessary to shift our underlying course methodology from the propensity to be monological to dialogical.

GENUINE DIALOGUE

I-Thou relationship is dialogical. But it is not quite that simple. We usually use the word *dialogue* to refer to individuals talking together, but five years after publishing *I and Thou* Buber described three types of communicating:

1. *Genuine Dialogue*—"Whether spoken or silent . . . each of the participants really has in mind the other or others in their present and particular being and turns to them with the intention of establishing a living mutual relation[ship] between himself and them."
2. *Technical Dialogue*—"[That communication] which is prompted solely by the need of objective understanding."
3. *Monologue Disguised as Dialogue*—"[That situation] in which two or more [persons], meeting in space, speak . . . in strangely tortuous and circuitous ways and yet imagine they have escaped the torment of being thrown back on their own resources."[9]

Neither monological nor dialectical, genuine dialogue is situated at the borders of what Martin Buber called the "interhuman realm" (*Zwischenmenschlichkeit*). For Buber, educating happens through relational events. "Relationship educates," he writes.[10] Instead of focusing on teacher-centered or student-centered models of instruction, Buber would concentrate our attention on the relationships between student and teacher, and teacher, student, and course material.

In every genuine dialogue, there are three, not two, voices. The first is the voice of the person speaking, the second is the voice of the other person in the dialogue, and the third is the voice of the relationship itself, which inspires and speaks through the first two voices.

As Buber and Russian literary critic Mikhail Bakhtin argued, the human sciences are phenomenologically and dialogically constructed. Instead of educating students about "voiceless things," we should strive to give our subjects a voice, to let the texts we use speak directly to each student's life stance. Education occurs "on the far side of the subjective, on this side of the objective, on the narrow ridge, where I and Thou meet."[11]

In the monological sphere, the other is regarded as a thing among other things to be experienced and used. Dialogue becomes *genuine* when each of the participants is fully present to the other or others, openly attentive to all voices, and willfully nonjudgmental. Dialogue becomes *technical* when the need to understand something or gain information is the focal point of the exchange. Dialogue becomes *monologue* when one participant is only interested in imposing his or her point of view to the exclusion of all other views.

These distinctions affect the educational process practically and directly. Genuine dialogue between and among teacher, students, and course material is the product of four characteristics:

* *turning* unreservedly toward the other,
* *addressing* the other acceptingly,
* *listening* to the other attentively, and
* *responding* responsibly to the dialogical partner.

When these behaviors are mutually practiced, real learning happens.

The most fruitful classroom situation is one in which genuine dialogue—direct, honest, immediate, and mutual—happens all the way around. In this way, students and the teacher are together challenged to understand teachings, texts, and traditions more deeply and clearly. At the same time, students and the teacher are engaged by critical and creative self-understandings.

SPOKENNESS

Dialogical behaviors between persons in educational settings have no reducible meaning or content that can be analyzed. Dialogue is meaningful in itself. Trying to define its significance would be like attempting to define the meaning of a line of poetry, or of an artistic image, without referring to new explanatory metaphors. Although not measurable, the direct, reciprocal, present dialogical relationship between unique persons is necessary if the wholeness and uniqueness of a person is to emerge from the knowledge imparted.

Practicing genuine dialogue and making it a habit requires not just that we speak, but rather that we are *spoken through* our encounters in the classroom. In other words, we share with our students a striving for self-confirmation and build from this shared sense a dialogical language within which we can think, communicate, and create.

What impressed Buber most in his university studies in Vienna was not so much listening to lectures as participating in seminars. He found that the seminar form, as opposed to the lecture format, encouraged "free intercourse between teacher and students, the common interpretations of texts, in which the master at times took part with a rare humility, as if he too were learning something new, and the liberated exchange of question and answer in the midst of all scholastic fluency—all this disclosed to me, more intimately than anything that I read in a book, the true actuality of the spirit, as a 'between.'"[12]

Buber was affected at least as much by attending the theater because he saw in great plays the creation of relational meaning out of a human language addressed not just to an audience but to himself as a partner in the dialogue. "Speech here first," he writes, "in this world of fiction as fiction, won its adequacy; certainly it appeared heightened."[13] For Buber, the kind of direct address that genuine dialogue allows comes from such "speech-with-meaning," speech that joins us in a mutually encountered togetherness.

RELEARNING IDENTITY

In this brief summary of Buber's notions of I-Thou and I-It, we can draw out the implications of genuine I-Thou dialogue for the educational process. The underlying point, for both teachers and learners, is that each person is called on to *relearn* his or her identity. You, as teacher, relearn who you are; you, as student, relearn who you are. Neither is a solitary, self-contained individual. Instead, we become aware of ourselves as persons in relationship to one another.

T. S. Eliot begins his final major poem *Four Quartets* with a line from the Greek philosopher Heraclitus that is appropriate here: Although the Logos is common to all, the majority live as though by a private wisdom of their own.

What constitutes Logos for Heraclitus is born of a reciprocal and reciprocating sharing of knowledge. Private knowing, for Heraclitus, is replaced by meaningful speaking and responding that is common to both teacher and students.

When dialogue is practiced, education becomes a multi-sided event, not a one-sided experience.

Nigel Tubbs captures the need to relearn our classroom dynamics, writing: "The I-Thou relation, therefore, is implicitly a critique of, or a re-education in regard to, our taken-for-granted assumptions about ourselves and others. Buber implies that there is such an educative import to the I-Thou relation when he says that, when we are truly in relation, we 'enter a realm where the law of the point of view no longer holds' . . . and we must learn about ourselves and others all over again."[14] When learning occurs genuinely, one is not fixed within a point of view that inflexibly judges other points of view. Rather, we take a dialogical stand, an entirely new and open perspective, in relation to who or what is being encountered.

LEARNING DIALOGICALLY

According to Maurice Friedman, a dialogical approach to knowing is "in direct contact in contrast to a detached subject's knowledge of an object."[15] We come to understand that our objective I-It knowledge is actually derived from I-Thou relationships. This means that in our approach to the human sciences as a whole, we must be concerned with the dialectical alternation between I-Thou knowing and I-It knowledge.

We must become more sensitive to and aware of the dialectical switching our classrooms undergo between these two primary words, from Thou to It and back again, and to understand how to elicit genuine dialogue from the information we are teaching.

A dialogical pedagogy, Friedman suggests, is an approach to becoming authentically human that is founded on the ontology of the between—the recognition that we become unique persons only in dialogue with other persons. The value of the dialogue is not found in either one or the other of the partners, nor in both added together, but in their interaction. Knowledge happens just as dialogue happens in relationship between, and not within, the individual participants in the dialogue.

POINTS TO REMEMBER

For Buber, there are two ways of learning: I-Thou (dialogical knowing) and I-It (individual knowledge).

- There are only two basic life-stands: I-Thou (two-sided) and I-It (one-sided).
- The four main elements of dialogue are: turning, addressing, listening, and responding.
- Buber carefully distinguishes between genuine dialogue, technical dialogue, and monologue disguised as dialogue.
- Practicing genuine dialogue includes relearning one's identity through reciprocity.
- Every genuine dialogue includes three voices: the speaker's, the listener's, and the voice of the dialogue itself.

NOTES

1. Martin Buber, *Between Man and Man*, trans. Ronald Gregor Smith (New York: The Macmillan Company, 1948), 102.

2. Martin Buber, *Philosophical Interrogations*, ed. Sydney and Beatrice Rome (New York: Holt, Rinehart, 1964), 67.

3. Martin Buber, *I and Thou*, trans. Ronald Gregor Smith, 2nd edition (New York: Charles Scribner's Sons, 1937/1958), 7. Unless otherwise noted, all references to *I and Thou* will be to the Smith translation.

4. The German for "I-Thou"—*Ich-Du*—has been translated in two ways. Ronald Gregor Smith, in his 1937 translation, uses the phrase I-Thou, which Buber personally agreed with. Later, in 1970, Walter Kaufmann translated *Ich-Du* as I-You because he believed that "I-Thou" gave readers the presumption that Buber was referring only to God. In fact, the word *Du* has more weight and is more accurate because it was rarely spoken in Buber's time. *Du*—the German "Thou"—was only used to address people toward whom one felt very close, and to describe a relationship that has a past, a present, and potential for a future.

5. *Haltung* refers to a person's stance in the world. It is reflected by the difference between two primary, or grounding, words (*grundworte*) that one speaks: I-Thou and I-It. But the translation "attitude," used by Smith and Kaufmann, is too psychologically oriented. The German word *Haltung* is more relational. It refers to the way I associate myself to what is present with me, that is my basic bearing, or life-orientation.

6. Buber, *I and Thou*, 59.

7. Buber, *I and Thou*, 11.

8. Buber, *I and Thou*, 3.

9. Martin Buber, *Between Man and Man*, 19.

10. Martin Buber, *A Believing Humanism*, trans. Maurice Freidman (New York: Simon and Schuster, 1969), 98.

11. Buber, *Between Man and Man*, 204.

12. Martin Buber, *Meetings*, ed. Maurice Friedman (Chicago: Open Court, 1973), 30–31.

13. Buber, Meetings, 30–31.

14. Nigel Tubbs, *Philosophy of the Teacher* (Oxford: Blackwell Publishing, 2005), 109.

15. Maurice Friedman, in *Dialogically Speaking: Maurice Friedman's Interdisciplinary Humanism*, ed. Kenneth Kramer (Eugene, Ore.: Pickwick Publications, 2011), 116.

Chapter Two

Buber's Method of Inclusion

What is to be done? To accomplish anything, Buber says: "You shall not withhold yourself."[1] Rather than withdrawing into oneself, rather than standing apart, we need to enter into respectful and direct relationships with others. One's life stance—one's basic attitude and self-image—is formed through dynamic interactions between the interhuman and social realms. The direction of a person's life shifts and is reformed in response to the unique differences of the other.

NOT QUITE A FULL PARTNERSHIP

In 1923, Ernst Simon—Buber's close friend—sharply criticized his teaching practices. He was especially critical of the way that Buber conducted a seminar in a reciprocal I-Thou style, as if participants shared full equality with the teacher. Simon wrote that in the seminar, "there developed a partly hysterical, somewhat shameless barrage of questions" along with a "psychological slopping around." Simon said to Buber: These eruptions were caused because "you have given no thought to your *audience*."[2]

In other words, Simon was asking Buber if there are limits to a dialogical pedagogy. Are there special circumstances that make genuine dialogue difficult if not impossible between teacher and student? If the goal of education as dialogue is to foster a student's growth through genuine encounters between I and Thou, can the relationship between teacher and student ever be fully mutual?

Buber's response, in the words of Maurice Friedman, to this question is as follows:

The teacher makes himself the living selection of the world, which comes in his person to meet, draw out, and form the pupil. In this meeting, the teacher puts aside the will to dominate and the will to enjoy the pupil that threaten "to stifle the growth of his blessings." The teacher is able to educate the pupils whom he finds before him only if he is able to build real mutuality between himself and them. This mutuality can come into existence only if the [student] trusts the teacher and knows that he is really there for him. [3]

INCLUSION

The key component of the pedagogic relationship is inclusion (*Umfassung*). Inclusion in this case means "making present," an act of imagining what the other person is thinking, feeling, and experiencing without surrendering one's own stand. Inclusion is beyond what is traditionally expected of students. It is an additional quality of responsibility and consciousness, and is specifically required of the teacher for a genuine dialogue to take place.

Kalmon Yaron, director of the Martin Buber Institute for Adult Education at the Hebrew University of Jerusalem, writes that "Buber's most original contribution to education is the application of his dialogical principle—and especially the element of inclusion—to the pedagogical realm." [4]

In "Education," Buber wrote that "the educator who practices the experiences of the other side and stands firm in it, experiences two things together, first that [she or he] is limited by otherness, and second that [she or he] receives grace by being bound to the other." [5] Offering to the students the world of genuine dialogue, the teacher comes in person to meet and to draw forth the students in new ways. To do this, teachers must learn to act from the heart of dialogue, which is the practice of inclusion.

In making the other present, of course, you too must be fully present. Todd Perreira describes Buber's insight of "making present" in a vivid image:

> We've all had the experience of walking along the sidewalk and, to avoid running into someone who is about to cross our path, we move off to the right side to allow the person to pass. But much to our bewilderment, this person has also moved off to the right side and suddenly you are both in danger of running into one another. Quickly, you move to the left side and at the very same instant so does the other person. Now you must both stop and smile awkwardly while one waits for the other to make the first move and pass. This is precisely what describes for me the ideal relationship between a professor and a student. [6]

In this image, a potential for confrontation becomes a dance between two people with the same agenda and turns into a learning exchange.

A teacher needs to be aware of the student's situated motives and intentions, of how the world is viewed from "over-there." Thus, inclusion requires a leap in perspective from the teacher's side of relationship to the student's side. It means being able to concretely imagine (as much as possible) what the student perceives.[7]

BOLDLY SWINGING

Inclusion seems like a contradiction. While we must hold our ground of subjectivity—Who would I be, after all, if I didn't have a subjective experience?—we also are compelled to go out and meet the other. How does this occur?

Maurice Friedman coined the term of "a bold imaginative swinging" to describe how we can traverse this duality of the subjective mind and understanding the genuine other.

Simply put, to boldly swing from one side of the relationship to the other without giving up one's stand "means seeing through the eyes of the other and experiencing the other's side of the relationship *without* ceasing to experience the relationship from one's own side."[8] It is the combination of a willing imagination and a temporary suspension of one-sided speech.

The capacity to boldly swing involves two nearly simultaneous movements: swinging *over* to the other's side, and then bringing *back* to one's own side as much of the other's situation as can be gleaned. Thomas A. Tweed points to the importance of trying to imagine the students' perspective when he writes:

> Teaching at its best means finding students where they are, and in that sense, and other senses, pedagogy is often about moving across. Although instructors never have final or complete success, they try to imaginatively transport themselves to the chairs around the seminar table and the inclined rows of seats in the lecture hall. And teaching involves other sorts of crossings: it means—to appeal to an overused phrase—"active learning," students engaged in making and sharing of knowledge, thereby crossing the line between learner and teaching.[9]

FIRST DAY OF CLASS

Buber describes an event that every teacher experiences—the first day of class.

> For the first time a young teacher enters a class independently, no longer sent by the training college to prove his efficiency. The class before him is like a mirror of [humankind], so multiform, so full of contradictions, so inaccessible.

> [The teacher] feels "these [students]—I have not sought them out; I have been put here and have to accept them as they are—but not as they now are in this moment, no, as they *really* are, as they can become."[10]

This is a key moment for any teacher. All of the teacher's training flashes across his or her mind. A decision has to be made. Of course, the students are noisy and easily distracted. The teacher may even be tempted to address disruptive forms of behavior; but then the teacher's eyes encounter a student's face that strikes the teacher with openness. The teacher feels how the student feels.

> It is not a beautiful face nor particularly intelligent; but it is a real face, or rather, the chaos preceding the cosmos of a real face. On it he reads a question which is something different from the general curiosity, "Who are you? Do you know something that concerns me? Do you bring me something? What do you bring?"[11]

In this process, the teacher is able to place him- or herself in the position of the student who brings these perceived questions because the teacher shares these questions and apprehensions. They can connect on this human level. One way to let students know that they are being included is to ask a question of them with genuine curiosity, especially one that elicits a story.

A small matter in and of itself, an earnestly asked question from teacher to students momentarily suspends the educational agenda and helps to make the students present. This act brings about a recognition of the others' uniqueness and viewing the other persons as meaningful. Professor Brian Coppola says: "The importance of the teacher's ability to elicit a story from one's student, which attracted full-class attention, should not be overlooked. Stories—of all types and genres—stimulate relational learning."[12]

ONE-SIDED INCLUSION

The teacher-student relationship does not rest on a necessity for full mutuality. Rather, the teacher is more often asked to "enclose" or "embrace" students. Ernst Simon sums up Buber's characterization of the teacher-student relationship as an I-Thou without full mutuality, writing that:

> The teacher has to understand both himself and the student, but for the student it is not enough to understand himself. Moreover, though the student may and should understand the teacher's words, he can never be expected to understand the teacher's being in its full dimensions. The true teacher will understand this not-being-understood by his pupil . . . [and] will "embrace" the whole situation with its two poles; his own and that of the pupil. The latter is concerned only with himself.[13]

Inherently unequal, the teacher-student relationship expects the practice of inclusion on the part of the teacher only. The teacher must be aware of the ever-changing needs of students.

At the core of teacher-student relationship is what Buber called the event of "one-sided inclusion." By imagining oneself from the point of view of a student, by feeling how the student is affected, a teacher gains insight into what is and is not needed. Only then does he or she begin to comprehend the real limits and challenges of the teaching situation.

The challenge for the teacher is to recognize how challenged the students are. The students are challenged to relinquish control of the conversation. They rely on the teacher to include their viewpoints in the educational process. It is the teacher's responsibility to be trustworthy (to demonstrate knowledge of the material along with including the students' perspectives) and to trust the students (to be motivated and engaged with the material).

This power imbalance between teacher and students almost requires the dialogical method to overcome it, that is, to bring about trust between them. The need for a teacher to practice one-sided inclusion without disempowering the student is a natural consequence of a dialogical pedagogy.

WHAT THE TEACHER LEARNS

In the dialogical approach to education, the teacher learns along with the students. In the words of Ezra Pound, "There is no [teacher] who knows so much about, let us say, a passage [in] . . . *The Odyssey* that he can't learn something by re-reading it WITH his students, not merely TO his students."[14] What the teacher learns emerges through itself. More than information, more than conceptual data, ever again teachers come to know the unique concreteness of becoming human.

Along this vein, Buber does not want to imply that no real dialogue is possible between the teacher and student. He writes:

> However much the teacher is superior to the pupil in experience, there is, nonetheless, something that the former can learn from the latter: this is the personal experiences that the pupil has had and that he communicates directly or indirectly. Every teacher who has ears and a heart will willingly listen to such reports, which are irreplaceable because they are grounded in individuals; and he will incorporate them in his manifold world-and-life-experience; but he will also help the pupil to advance confidently from the individual experience that he has now had to an organic knowledge of the world and life. Such an interchange, although it cannot be a full one, I call, in spite of all, a dialogical one.[15]

In the classroom, "we live in the currents of universal reciprocity,"[16] and even though this reciprocity is limited, it is a reciprocity of genuine dialogue.

Anthropologist Mira Z. Amiras writes:

> It is the students who provide their own unique experiences and insights that
> make the point and prove instructive. They begin, however, with only their
> own experience and perspective, often mistaking these for some larger or
> universal "truth." Providing multiple lenses through which to examine the
> world around them changes their understanding of their own experience and
> allows them to perceive themselves and the world around them from a more
> empathetic, analytical, and ultimately holistic perspective. [17]

IN BUBER'S CLASS

To exemplify what Buber means by inclusion, it is helpful to consider a
personal account from Buber's student, Mishael Caspi, a retired professor of
religion, Judaic studies and Islamic civilization. "My earliest memory of
Professor Martin Buber was at a seminar he gave in the teacher training
college which he created in the '50s in Israel."[18] Mishael recounts:

> I remember in a class of about seven or eight, he talked about the book of
> Genesis and the creation of the world. With his smiling eyes and white beard,
> he talked in a way that bewildered me. Sometimes, I felt what he was saying
> was much beyond me.
> At one point, he said something about his concept of creation which I did not
> fully understand. I raised my hand and he stopped talking and asked me what I
> wanted to say. "I would very much like to know what your conception of the
> creation of the world is," I said. And try to understand, while I was raised in a
> very orthodox house, I had just finished my service in the army. Being a
> member of the Kibbutz, I was between Orthodoxy and a denial of all its
> teaching. So I really wanted to understand how other people view the creation.
> In a very beautiful Jewish way he said to me: "What is creation for you?" And
> I looked at him with surprise at the fact that he wanted to know from me what I
> wanted to know from him. I stuttered at first, and then I said: "I think that
> creation is to be a part of what is happening, a part of creation" (*ye-hi-dah Shel
> ha-Beri-ah*). And he shook his head and said: "No, no, no. It is to be together
> with creation" (*Ye-hi-dah, Ya-had im ha-Be-ri-ah*). It took me a long time to
> be able to understand the difference between "to be a part of" and "to be a part
> with." In many senses, I understood later on that Buber's response emphasized
> for me the whole concept of *I and Thou* in a very simple way. [19]

Buber's first response in the story is inclusion in action. He imagined Mishael's situation (one of uncertainty) and included his attitude (one of sincerity). Rather than responding immediately to Caspi with his own view of
creation (which he had done on other occasions), Buber first elicited Mishael's own understanding.

By crossing over to Mishael's side of their meeting, by concretely imagining what he was thinking and feeling, Buber gained insight into the situa-

tion of Mishael's question. This understanding, this concrete imagining of the other, in turn led Buber to an answer that met Mishael precisely where he was in his life, an answer that would continue to flower in Mishael's understanding. In many ways, Buber's inclusion of Mishael in his response was as much an answer to the question of creation as was his literal response. Like creation, education is being together and with.

RESPONSIBILITY

Responsibility to do what? Simply put, to say what is meant and do what is said. In the dialogue-centered classroom, both teachers and students can practice this when:

- responding to what addresses them in the situation;
- communicating everything that comes to mind, without being judgmental;
- having the courage, not only to address, but also to respond to the other;
- recognizing that meaningful learning arises through building a common situation together.

When discussing the impact of Buber's teaching, Mishael once said that Buber's philosophy of dialogue had influenced his entire teaching career. In response, when asked how he might characterize Buber's influence in a paragraph, he gave the following explanation.

> In 1953, at a Teacher Training College in Jerusalem, Professor Buber delivered a lecture about education and the role of the teacher. He stated that a teacher is not just a spiritual guide, but also someone who challenges his students to think, to be able to ask questions, and to be able to dialogue together with others. He then emphasized that a dialogue is a model for communicating ideas and worldviews, but he included in this communication mode another aspect which he called "responsibility." He saw it as the focal point.

Buber's remarks had a profound effect of Mishael. He writes: "I opened my heart and understood that my role as a teacher-professor is to point to certain ideas and thoughts, and let the students commence a long dialogue in which no definite answer is given. Rather, ideas and questions are pointed to through which one learns, understands, and respects the other and at the same time develops oneself as a human."[20]

POINTS TO REMEMBER

Buber's primary method of inclusion embodies listening to the other (person/ text) both from your side and by sympathetically experiencing the other's side.

- Inclusion is the practice of empathetically encountering the other person's thoughts, feelings, and experiences.
- One-sided inclusion occurs when only one person in the conversation is able to practice full mutuality.
- Practicing one-sided inclusion allows teachers to more engagingly and accurately communicate with students.
- An essential element in educational dialogue is the need for responding responsibly to what is said and read.

NOTES

1. Martin Buber, *Pointing the Way*, trans. Martin Friedman (New York: Schocken Books, 1957), 109.

2. Ernst Simon to Martin Buber, November 2, 1923, in *The Letters of Martin Buber*, ed. Nahum M. Glatzer and Paul Mendes-Flohr (New York: Syracuse University Press, 1991), 307.

3. Maurice Friedman, *Encounter on the Narrow Ridge: A Life of Martin Buber* (New York: Paragon House, 1991), 186.

4. Kalmon Yaron, "Martin Buber," *Prospects: The Quarterly Review of Comparative Education* 23, no. 1/2 (1993): 135–46.

5. Martin Buber, *Between Man and Man*, trans. Ronald Gregor Smith, 101.

6. Todd Perreira, January 25, 1995, letter to Outstanding Professor Committee at San José State University.

7. Martin Buber, *The Knowledge of Man*, trans. with introduction by Maurice Friedman (New York: Harper & Row, 1965) 70.

8. Maurice Friedman, *Religion and Psychology: A Dialogical Approach* (New York: Paragon House, 1992), 38.

9. Thomas A. Tweed, *Crossing and Dwelling: A Theory of Religion* (Cambridge, Mass: Harvard University Press, 2008), 180. I do not agree with Tweed when he writes that "In teaching as in research, the first step is reflexive positioning. The word *reflexive*, means 'turning back'; it is a turning back to the self and, I would add, to the community" (178). Just the opposite. The first step, I believe, is turning away from self-preoccupations and toward entering into relationship with students.

10. Buber, *Between Man and Man*, 112.

11. Buber, *Between Man and Man*, 112.

12. Professor Brian Coppola, who teaches organic chemistry at the University of Michigan, received Baylor University's 2012 Cherry Award for great teaching because his students learned more than the structure of compounds. "They learn how to connect themselves to knowledge to discover a story that's uniquely theirs. Relating chemistry to storytelling is just one of the things that make Doctor Coppola a great teacher." *New York Times*, April 15, 2012, 7. See also "U'-M's Brian Coppola wins national teaching award." http://www.ns.umich.edu/new/multimedia/videos/20156-u-ms-brian-coppola-wins-national-teaching-award.

13. Ernst Simon, "Martin Buber, The Educator," in *The Philosophy of Martin Buber*, ed. Paul Arthur Schilpp and Maurice Friedman (LaSalle, Ill.: Open Court, 1967), 571–72.

14. Ezra Pound, *ABC of Reading* (New York: New Directions, 1960), 85.

15. Martin Buber, *Philosophical Interrogations*, ed. Sydney and Beatrice Rome (New York: Holt, Rinehart, 1964), 66.

16. Martin Buber, *I and Thou*, trans. Walter Kaufmann (New York: Charles Scribner's Sons, 1970), 67.

17. Mira Z. Amiras, in an e-mail on February 27, 2012.

18. In 1949, Buber was invited to establish the Teachers' Institute for the Education of Adults. "He had no desire to establish just another teachers' institute, but saw in the new institute a unique opportunity to field test and implement his theory of education for a free and humanistic society which is devoid of propaganda and imposition." Joshua Weinstein, *Buber and Humanistic Education* (New York: Philosophical Library, 1975), 59.

19. Mishael Caspi, as told to the author and included in a slightly different form in Kenneth Kramer, *Martin Buber's* I and Thou, *Practicing Living Dialogue* (New York: Paulist Press, 2003), 193–94.

20. In an e-mail from Mishael Caspi to the author, October 11, 2011.

Chapter Three

Teaching as Unteaching

No matter how brilliant the professor or how fascinating and valuable the course, the learning-teaching process is, at its best, a function of *awakened attention*. Like it or not, if we want students to be excited by the significance of the subject matter, then its presentation must also be exciting. Does this suggest that a teacher should be passionate about the course? Yes. But even more importantly, it suggests that the way students are taught must also be impassioned.

AS THOUGH NOT DOING

One becomes uniquely and dialogically present whenever one is open to the ever-changing and always unprecedented uniqueness of each person. The act of stepping into direct relationship with others, from wholeness to wholeness, involves surrendering one's agenda and willingly being chosen by another.

In *I and Thou*, Buber describes this activity as "doing nothing: nothing separate or partial."[1] Being dialogically present, in other words, involves "not doing." Dialogue is an action-less action, one very similar to the Taoist understanding of *wu-wei*, of doingless-doing, or acting without being attached to the outcomes of the action.

Applying this Taoist understanding of *wu-wei* to teaching, Buber writes: "If the educator of our day has to act consciously he must nevertheless do it 'as though he did not.' That rising of the finger, that questioning glance, are his genuine doing. Through him the selection of the effective world reaches the pupil. He fails the recipient when he presents this selection to him with a gesture of interference."[2] *Unteaching* is necessary and complementary to teaching. Larry Fader writes, "One possible reconciliation of this education conundrum: to learn from the teacher to be free of the teacher."[3]

23

Chapter 3

ATTITUDE AND ACTIVITY

Unteaching means letting go of the controls that restrict the teaching process. It is as much an attitude as activity. Unteaching moves the class beyond the ordinary teaching models, in which the educational flow is initiated by the teacher and received by the students.

Unteaching is a dimension of the teaching method just as an echo is a dimension of a symphony. It shifts from monological discourse to dialogical interaction. It is less interested in the absorption of knowledge than it is in learning through participation. The "un" in unteaching refers to an attitude or style that expands the teaching context to include and involve students in the process. It is neither teacher directed nor student directed. Instead, it lets our relationship to the material do the teaching.

The unteaching teacher can relinquish sole responsibility for the imparting of knowledge, can stimulate others to join in the teaching process, and can encourage everyone to remain open to the material in a self-motivated way. The skill and the acumen of the teacher and the inherent abilities of the student are two sides of the unteaching coin. It is on a precarious narrow ridge between the two that genuine pedagogical creativities occur.

THE FUNNEL AND THE PUMP

Buber characterizes two common and contrasting approaches to education with the metaphor of a funnel and that of a pump. The funnel suggests a mostly traditional view of education where the teacher (the one who knows) pours material into the minds of students. This approach lacks spontaneity and freedom.

Meanwhile, the pump reflects a more progressive view of education in which the teacher's role is to facilitate the unfolding potential within his or her students, as if teaching them to pump water from a well deep within. This method removes a necessary facilitation and guidance provided by the teacher.

For Buber, each of these approaches is deficient. Each method is restricted by a one-sided approach that ultimately fails to address the learning situation as a whole. Through combinations of ineptness, ignorance, and laziness (on both sides of the teaching-learning arc), students' sense of participation dwindles.

Buber rejected the idea that education means merely the acquisition of knowledge as well as the idea that education is only the transformation of a student's worldviews. Such views of education, he believed, simply perpetuate the spread of the It world, in which objectifying, possessing, and achieving are the main goals. Buber's philosophy of dialogue addresses this issue by providing a third method.

A THIRD ALTERNATIVE

In the dialogical classroom, education is characterized by reciprocity. In a reciprocal classroom, the teacher and the course material come alive with a personal immediacy that draws students forth. This is not a self-directed or other-directed process, but dialogue-directed learning.

Debates on educational theory and practice usually focus on the fundamental question: Should education elicit the self-directed development of ideas from within individual students, or should it impose an other-directed formation of thoughts from without? From Plato to Jerome Bruner, educators have supported either the *subjective* side of knowledge (in which knowledge develops out of a student's own creative powers) or the *objective* side (in which knowledge is imposed from without).

Neither the subjective side nor the objective side is complete in itself. Convinced that the real choice does not lie between personal relativity on the one hand or authoritarian imposition on the other, Buber proposed that real teaching-and-learning is a *dialogical activity* in which the educator recognizes each student as a unique person with a distinctive perspective, and in which students encounter and participate with the educator as someone who is relatable to and present for them.

Buber's vision for education is a transformation of the ways in which people relate to each other. But this end is not a goal. For genuine education to occur, the student-teacher relationship must be grounded in genuine dialogue at the outset. Buber writes:

> Here, if anywhere, it is impossible to teach or to learn without living. The teachings must not be treated as a collection of knowable material; they resist such treatment. Either the teachings live in the life of a responsible human being, or they are not alive at all. The teachings do not center in themselves; they do not exist for their own sake. They refer to, they are directed toward the deed. In this connection the concept of "deed" does not, of course, connote "activism," but life that realizes the teachings in the changing potentialities of every hour.[4]

RELATIONSHIP EDUCATES

Buber distinguished between and recognized the relationship among three dimensions of dialogue: acceptance, affirmation, and confirmation. The interplay between these relational dynamics results in the realization that it is not the instructor who educates, but the educational process itself. The teacher-content-student conversation provides an exchange of felt ideas.

In genuine interactions, we move from a generic acceptance (I accept you as a person like myself) to a specific affirmation of one's unique self (I affirm you in your difference from myself) to a confirmation of the other (I trustingly validate you as a dialogical partner both now and in the future). Confirmation is mutual when partners are able to imagine what the other person is thinking, feeling, and wishing.

Inner growth is not accomplished through self-exploration alone but through the realization that the other is unique and mutually present as well. A distancing must occur in order for true dialogue to exist because it is in the space between people that each person becomes a self. When we make the other fully present and know that we are made present by the other, there is reciprocity of affirmation and confirmation.

The teacher's listening and questioning search into the unspoken areas between teacher and students. This elicits the expression of that which was heretofore inexpressible. Real teaching occurs when participating with students in genuine I-Thou relationships. Directly engaging students in honest dialogue, the teacher-student relationship is what creates the playing field on which fully internalized, highly impactful education occurs.

THE NARROW RIDGE

Buber characterized his own position in relation to others as standing on the insecure "narrow ridge" between conflicting absolutes, between subjectivity and objectivity, right and wrong, between life and death itself. On this narrow ridge, where there is no certainty of expressible knowledge, a space opens where real encounter between humans occurs. Genuine dialogue occurs on the narrow ridge between absolute truths.

Buber once remarked: "I do not accept any absolute formulas for living. . . . No preconceived code can see ahead to everything that can happen in a [person's] life. As we live, we grow, and our beliefs change. They must change. So I think we could live with this constant discovery. We should be open to this adventure in heightened awareness of living. We should stake our whole existence on our willingness to explore and experience."[5]

In Buber's dialogical approach, real learning is neither "teacher-down" nor "student-up" but intersubjective and interhuman. Real learning is a two-sided, address-response event that happens on the "narrow ridge" of genuine dialogue. This metaphor illustrates a kind of teaching that does not rest on the broad upland of "sure statements" or "sure knowledge," but instead happens in the dialogue between all the either-or propositions of the intellectual world.[6]

The narrow ridge is "no 'happy middle' which ignores the reality of the paradox and contradiction in order to escape from the suffering they produce. It is rather a paradoxical unity of what one usually understands only as alternatives—I *and* Thou, love *and* justice, dependence *and* freedom . . . good *and* evil, unity *and* duality."[7]

INTERSUBJECTIVITY

On the dialogical narrow ridge, students, teachers, and the content studied are related in an intersubjective, interpretive community. The term "intersubjective" refers to the self and voice, the speaking and listening, the perspectives and experiences of each person, or subject, that we address. It implies a willingness to remain open to learning and changing in each new dialogical interaction. It implies that all parties share both a sense of agency and a unique perspective.

Such an intersubjective educational community is not comprised of a knowing subject (the teacher) and known objects (the content and the students). Rather, teacher, students, and content are related as co-creative subjects in a hermeneutical conversation. Subject matter, in this educational *praxis*, is presented and discussed as a living Thou with its own unique voice and perspective. Interpretive understanding becomes an open-ended inquiry. Rather than searching for objective "truth," the intersubjective educational community is characterized by its ongoing search for existential trust.

This kind of educational community develops existential trust because walking the narrow ridge of dialogue is extremely challenging and requires it. The teacher, for example, wants neither to lose his or her voice nor to impede or in any way squelch the voice of the students. The students feel likewise, and the text at hand seems imposing and monological.

How can an intersubjective dialogue generate knowing between and among the teacher, the students, and the text/content given all of these limitations? What specific actions and attitudes are required of the teacher to coax genuine dialogue out of a learning situation like this?

Joshua Guilar indicates that the teacher, whom he calls the "up-to-date scholar," sets and guides the educational community by modeling authority and vulnerability, courage, and humility. "The major charge," he writes, "of the dialogic instructor is to engage students in content while creating context for a conversation that [is] hermeneutical or intersubjective."[8] He pictures teaching styles existing on a continuum ranging from an autocratic instructional style to an overly permissive style.

Buber emphasized the necessity of giving students direction, a striking distinction between dialogic enabling and the permissive and autocratic styles. Buber addressed this element of teaching specifically: "The teacher must show the pupil the direction. He must point the way. But the pupil must make the journey himself. And you show someone the direction only when he wants to go the same way—the way of realization, of throwing his whole self into the journey."[9]

In response, a teacher asked, "But surely it is not enough merely to point the direction? What about the agreed values which tell our pupils how to behave?" Buber replied quietly: "Let us try to understand what we mean when we use this word 'values.' Can absolute values be formulated at all? I wish I could do so. . . . I do not like talking about principles. I prefer to discuss different situations. But these are not fixed. Perhaps the situation of today will not be the same as the situation of tomorrow."[10] According to Buber, values, like a direction of movement in one's life, must arise out of one's personal wholeness in response to the invitation to dialogue that presents itself.

PERSONAL WHOLENESS

Personal wholeness is not a once-and-for-all state of being. Rather than a static pre-condition or the content of a belief, realized wholeness is a direction of movement that comes and goes in particular concrete moments. Wholeness, the heart of intersubjective education, requires both choosing to enter relationship and being chosen by one who also chooses to enter relationship. In other words, dialogical wholeness involves surrender and action, grace and will. The word *wholeness* best characterizes the direction we are called to give to our students. Wholeness is actualized in genuine moments of engagement, withholding nothing, leaving nothing out.

It is our job as teachers to direct students toward wholeness—toward attentiveness to their partnership in the dialogue. If we do this job well, students will apprehend and remember the knowledge we are trying to impart, or the text we are trying to understand, because they would have encountered it as a partner in the dialogical community and will have contributed that encounter to the dialogical learning community as a whole.

Even if a teacher lacks the ability to move students with stirring words of inspiring certitude, Buber notes: "The unpretentious and most important ability is still theirs, to advise, to exhort, to guide. They set us ever in the presence of the searching beams of truth. They lead in that they teach. Theirs is the secret history of the world."[11]

Why secret? Because at its core, teaching on the narrow ridge embodies relational trust. This is trust that: recognizes no student is uneducable; acknowledges genuine relationships are two-sided, beyond only our control; and asks us to have the courage to meet the other, to overcome existential mistrust and respond responsibly to the other. Relational trust is central to human existence and expresses itself through dialogue and confirmation.

DRAWING FORTH

If we become attuned to listening—keenly listening—as we stand on the narrow ridge, we can hear not two, but three voices in every genuine dialogue: the speakers' and the voice of the relationship. This is why it is vitally important to realize that it is not the teacher who educates but the dialogical relationship itself between and among teacher and students that educates.

The dialogue is in itself educative because in the process the students' isolating armor melts and they open up to engage the course materials. Buber insisted, according to Joshua Weinstein, that "it is the responsibility of each person to determine for himself the choice of his own destiny. He believed that the major task of education is to awaken in the pupils the desire to assume responsibility for their actions."[12]

The highest goal of teaching is the education of character. By character Buber did not mean a single function of personality, nor personality itself, but the total human (body, mind, spirit) being both now and as he or she will become. Buber's model teacher acts as if she or he is not teaching, is dedicated to the profession, respects the right of each student, is open to discuss opposing viewpoints, and strives to awaken in students the value of their own searching.

From the teacher's perspective: what are students searching for? And what is to be drawn forth from the students? Not just ideas, surely. Not just more information. What then?

The "speaking voice" of the students needs to be brought forth: the students' expression of ideas in the educational context. In the process of drawing-forth, the two-sided, I-Thou relationship between teacher and students educates.

It is almost as if in order to enter a genuine relationship with another, one needs to overcome the way one has been educated, the way one has been conditioned to "hear" only what is important, or necessary, to hear from the teacher's point of view and take note of what the teacher emphasizes. Much of what we have learned is framed into categorical points of view. Most of our encounters are lifted from their original, dialogical context and placed on the pedestal of objective discourse.

In the words of Maurice Friedman, "The student grows through her encounters with the person of the teacher and the voice of the writer. This means that no real learning takes place unless the student participates." Still, what is it precisely that the student participates in? To know this, "the student must encounter something really 'other' than herself before she can learn. Education as true dialogue must involve real contact between persons (student and student as well as student and teacher) and bring to light knowledge that is itself a product of this mutual contact."[13]

POINTS TO REMEMBER

Teaching becomes unteaching when one is able to let go of being one hundred percent in control of the class and allows oneself to be influenced and directed by the back-and-forth dynamic rhythm of intersubjectivity.

* Unteaching refers to the practice of allowing the dialogue to teach both student and teacher.
* This process cannot be described as teacher-centered or student-centered—it is dialogue-centered.
* Teaching intersubjectively allows ideas to emerge from the exchange between and among teacher, students, and teaching.
* The "narrow ridge" refers to any place where genuine dialogue occurs—between contrasting ideas.
* Ideally, the teacher addresses the whole student rather than the student as an object of the teacher's experience.

NOTES

1. Martin Buber, *I and Thou*, 76.
2. Martin Buber, *Between Man and Man*, trans. Ronald Gregor Smith (New York: The Macmillan Company, 1948), 90.
3. Larry Fader, *120'00": A Conversation with John Cage* (Maine: Nine Point Publishing, 2012), viii.
4. Martin Buber, *Israel and the World, Essays in a Time of Crisis* (New York: Schocken Books, 1948), 140.
5. Aubrey Hodes, *Martin Buber: An Intimate Portrait* (New York: Viking Press, 1971), 56.
6. Buber, *Between Man and Man*, 184.
7. Buber, *Israel and the World*, 17.
8. Joshua D. Guilar, "Intersubjectivity and Dialogic Instruction," *Radical Pedagogy* 8, no. 1 (2006). Retrieved December 21, 2011, from radicalpedagogy.icaap.org/content/issue8_1 .
9. Quoted in Hodes, *Martin Buber*, 124.
10. Hodes, *Martin Buber*, 124–25.
11. Martin Buber, *Mamre: Essays in Religion*, trans. Greta Hort (Westport, Conn.: Greenwood Press, 1946), 63.
12. Joshua Weinstein, *Buber and Humanistic Education* (New York: Philosophical Library, 1975), 52.
13. Maurice Friedman in association with David Damico, *Genuine Dialogue and Real Partnership: Foundations of True Community* (Bloomington, Ind.: Trafford Publishing, 2011), 65.

Chapter Four

The Broadest Frame:
Dialogue as Meta-Methodology

If teaching and learning involve dialogical interactions between teacher and student, a similar dialogical exchange holds between various disciplines and methodologies. Think, for instance, of the complex interpretive issues that are raised when a philosophical or theological approach is juxtaposed with psychological or anthropological ones. Can a common ground be found?

MULTIPLE METHODOLOGIES

When divergent methodologies encounter one another, dialogical interactivity can become a common ground where interpretations meet and engage one another. In the dialogical classroom, lectures and discussions clarify awareness of interactions between and within a plurality of disciplinary interpretations.

No matter how they are framed, academic studies utilize a plurality of methods: historical, sociological, anthropological, psychological, phenomenological, and philosophical. The approach taken here uses multiple lenses that are essential for the study of all human knowledge and interaction. This raises a highly relevant question: how are these multiple methods to be used? How can we apply the varieties of available methods in humanistic disciplines without privileging one over the others, without losing sight of the significant interactions between them? Is there another method that can offer assistance?

Different approaches lead to varied accounts. To mention just one example, consider the difficulty of defining the term *religion*. How can one arrive at a conclusive answer, especially when there are so many experts with differing views?

INTERPRETIVE FRAMES

William Paden suggests that "interpretation is not just the realm of nonscientific 'opinions' as opposed to solid facts, not just an elitist, academic pasttime, but the translation of what we observe into frames of meaning and thus part of the natural process of constructing the world," that is, "to *interpret* is to bring out the meaning of something that would not otherwise be clear."[1]

Most liberal arts are largely influenced by two interpretive frames: (1) the social scientific (e.g., anthropology, sociology, psychology), which offer an empirical, analytic study of religious data; and (2) the humanistic (e.g., philosophy, history, phenomenology), which offers a descriptive and structural study of the data.

It is not this particular arrangement of methodologies that will be addressed, but the mediating and integrating middle ground of dialogue as a meta-methodology that brings these groupings into conversation. The central issue is, how does dialogue as the broadest possible frame enable us to bridge and integrate these various methodologies?

From a comparativist's standpoint, for instance, how does one understand the word *religion*? The pivotal question is: *How can I best employ a diversity of methods in a way that both validates each approach on the one hand, and raises critical challenges to each method on the other hand?*

The co-existence of diverse descriptions is best facilitated by a dialogical matrix. Each discipline has a valid voice, in which methods are kept open to critical reflection and are clarified in a dialogical relationship with the others. The classroom is the framework, or "in between" space, in which existing methods, theories, and explanations encounter, challenge, clarify, and cross-reference each other.

PERFORMANCE FRAMEWORK

When we encounter multiple, conflicting methodologies, what we need is a clearly delineated performance framework or conversational space. In this space, we do not oversimplify, but instead allow each to have a full voice without imposing any single methodology on what is studied.

When we prioritize a single method, we become manacled by our own disciplinary predispositions. Yet, to benefit from the extraordinarily rich variety of approaches, the disciplinary apparatus, the subject matter, and the teacher need to create a context in which each can be heard. A multi-narrative, interactive, and dialogical classroom provides such a context.

Table 4.1.   Interpretive Frames

Social Sciences	Humanities
Anthropology	**Philosophy**
A vital impulse which, combined with intelligence, ensures survival.[a]	What the individual does with his own solitariness.[b]
Sociology	**History**
A unified system of beliefs and practices relative to sacred things.[c]	A historical cumulative tradition and the personal faith of humans.[d]
Psychology	**Phenom enology**
The feelings, acts, and experiences of individuals in their solitude.[e]	Something for which there is only one appropriate expression, *mysterium tremendum*.[f]

a. E. E. Evans-Pritchard, *Theories of Primitive Religion* (New York: Oxford University Press, 1968), 116. The fuller quote reads: "Therefore religion is not, as some have supposed, a product of fear, but an assurance, and insurance, against fear. Ultimately it is a product of an instinctual urge, a vital impulse which, combined with intelligence, insures [humanity's] survival."

b. Alfred North Whitehead, *Religion in the Making* (New York: New American Library, 1926), 16. The fuller quote reads: "Religion is what the individual does with his own solitariness; and if you are never solitary, you are never religious."

c. Emile Durkheim, *Elementary Forms of the Religious Life* (New York: Macmillan, 1915), 62. The fuller quote reads: "A religion is a unified system of beliefs and practices relative to sacred things, that is to say, things set apart and forbidden—beliefs and practices which unite into one single moral community called a church, all those who adhere to them."

d. Wilfred Cantwell Smith, *The Meaning and End of Religion* (New York: Fortress Press, 1962), 175. The fuller quote reads: "Religion can more rewardingly, more truly, be conceived [as] an historical 'cumulative tradition,' and the personal faith of [humans]."

e. William James, *The Varieties of Religious Experience* (New York: Longmans, Green & Co., 1902), 31–32. The fuller quote reads: "Religion . . . shall mean for us the feelings, acts, and experiences of individual [humans] in their solitude, so far as they apprehend themselves to stand in relation to whatever they may consider the divine."

f. Rudolf Otto, *The Idea of the Holy* (New York: Oxford University Press, 1958), 4, 12, 24. The fuller quote reads: "Religion is not exclusively contained and exhaustively comprised in any series of 'rational' assertions; and it is well worth while to attempt to bring the relation of the different 'moments' of religion to one another. . . . If we do so we shall find we are dealing with something for which there is only one appropriate expression, '*mysterium tremendum*'" [hidden, esoteric, beyond conception, Wholly Other]."

Diana Eck suggests a similar methodology. Eck describes her own teaching as "neither objectivist nor subjectivist, but . . . dialogical," meaning that it includes differences of opinion and reflects on the transformative potential of learning. Of the give-and-take of dialogue, Eck writes: "[Dialogue] does not mean that we will agree, but only that we will understand more clearly and that we will begin to replace ignorance, stereotype, even prejudice, with relationship. It is the language of mutuality, not of power."[2]

According to Eck, a two-way language of real encounter—"meeting, exchange, traffic, criticism, reflection, reparation, renewal"—is the basis for navigating through diversities. She describes the goal as follows: "We do not enter into dialogue with the dreamy hope that we will all agree, for the truth is we probably will not. We do not enter into dialogue to produce an agreement, but to produce real relationship, even friendship, which is premised upon mutual understanding, not agreement."[3] A dialogical approach embodies various kinds of conversations. In a dialogical conversation between the varieties of approaches, we allow the discipline frames to associate themselves in dynamically interwoven clusters of voices.

OPEN TO WHAT'S NEW

The kinds of comparative dialogues that Diana Eck describes (including listening, reading, reflecting, talking, and challenging) can be likened to games that are already under way and yet are always open to new players (new phenomena and new interpreters). Since interdisciplinary dialogue can seem like a game, it has been suggested that these conversations need a structure or a set of rules to guide them. Instead of hard rules, interdisciplinary dialogue includes four principles:

1. It is interactively generated, for not only does each participant have an equal voice, but the conversation itself has a voice; that is, the conversation is the subject as much as it is about the subject.
2. It is listening-oriented, for one is required not only to speak but also to release into the concrete uniqueness of the other, to hear spoken content and unspoken attitudes, tones, and assumptions.
3. It is question-generated, for one is called to listen and also to express one's own self-understanding, to clarify, restate, and apply the common subject matter.
4. It is meaning-oriented, for not only is the conversation occasioned by the listening and speech-with-meaning of its present participants, but it remains open to new members, to new methods, and to new meanings that are not imposed from outside, but that emerge from the conversation itself.

The dialogical domain is a meta-methodological practice both open to and responsible for the various voices, disciplines, and methods involved in the humanities and social sciences. Its openness allows that which has not yet been expressed or completely articulated to take a recognizable form in the ongoing dialogue. It encourages us to be responsible for applying our critical and comparative understandings to that which is expressed.

THE LEARNING COMMUNITY AND DIVERSITY

Effective teaching and learning create a space for excited communication between teachers and students. However, a genuine educational community cannot be founded simply on shared values and beliefs. What brings a group of learners together is a desire to grow intellectually and expand perspectives. For this to occur, each member needs to interact respectfully with the unique presence of the others.

The learning community is the group of people who are willing to be present to and for each other; it necessarily recognizes and openly discusses multiple points of view. Diversity is not a difficulty to be overcome. A learning community's numerous viewpoints provide the material for continuous dialogue. Each person brings something quite concrete and unique into the communal relationship. Open-mindedness to others and new ideas, honesty, and willingness to change are more valuable to educational growth than like-mindedness.

This type of genuine community is not an end point, but a direction of movement, a reality that we try to build in every situation. Parker J. Palmer writes that when teaching is at its best, it evokes an educational community in which:

- We invite *diversity* into our community not because it is politically correct but because diverse viewpoints are demanded by the manifold mysteries of great things.
- We embrace *ambiguity* not because we are confused or indecisive but because we understand the inadequacy of our concepts to embrace the vastness of great things.
- We welcome *creative conflict* not because we are angry or hostile but because conflict is required to correct our biases and prejudices about the nature of great things.
- We practice *honesty* not only because we owe it to one another but because to lie about what we have seen would be to betray the truth of great things.
- We experience *humility* not because we have fought and lost but because humility is the only lens through which great things can be seen—and once we have seen them, humility is the only posture possible.
- We become *free* men and women through education not because we have privileged information but because tyranny in any form can be overcome only by invoking the grace of great things.[4]

THE HEART OF THE MATTER

Teaching and learning as multidisciplinary dialogue occurs when we are fully present and not withholding what we find important for fear of being judged. To the extent that one judges the other, real learning cannot occur. When we have the courage not only to address but also to respond honestly to the other, we recognize that speech-with-meaning arises in the process of building together a common world.

Here's the heart of the matter: teaching and learning flow between unique persons in an I-Thou structure of honest openness that preserves, yet dynamically overcomes, their separateness. Educative dialogue cannot be located within any one of the participants, but rather is found in their *betweenness*, in the interhuman reality. The realm of the between is not a location in the middle of two poles, nor is it the mathematical sum of each part. Rather, the between signifies a *place* (mutuality) and calls for an *interaction* (dialogue).

The interhuman realm of the between flourishes when the passion and activity of one person intertwines with the passion and activity of another. Each person, in the process, influences and challenges the other. It is here that real education occurs. Accordingly, the basic movement of genuine dialogue, and thus of education itself, is a truly reciprocal conversation in which teacher and students are partners.

The words of Wilfred Cantwell Smith reinforce Buber's central educational insight:

> The traditional form of Western scholarship in the study of other [religious traditions] was that of an impersonal presentation of an "it." The first great innovation in recent times has been the personalization of the faiths observed, so that one finds a discussion of a "they." Presently, the observer becomes personally involved, so that the situation is one of a "we" talking about a "they." The next step is a dialogue where "we" talk to "you." If there is listening and mutuality, this may become that "we talk with 'you.'" The culmination of the process is when "we all" are talking with each other about "us."

In response to Smith's insight, Todd Perreira says:

> I have this sense that a lot of influential scholars were reading Buber back then. He seems to have really struck a chord with many who shared his fear of a world dominated by an instrumentalist rationalism, one which was bent on converting the world into a mere object (for consumption) and legitimized under the banner of democracy and the "rights of man." But what good are human rights without any thought to human responsibility?[5]

CONFLICTING METHODS

Dialogically speaking, different pairs of methodological voices are not just contradictory but mutually supportive, mutually critical, and collaboratively creative. Each is a functional part of the conversation and is brought forth in the interplay between conflicting positions in multi-disciplinary networks.

Opposites implicate each other. *Implicate*, while it indicates that each position is unique and in its own way true, also highlights how different positions can clarify and challenge unique elements of each other. To make this happen, the teacher creates a conversational context in which there is an awareness of and a respect for the plurality of methods by which phenomena are studied.

However, how does one (or can one?) avoid a narrow absolutism on the one hand, or a broad relativism on the other? If each theory, each methodology, is given full voice in the educational process, are there any criteria for choosing among competing, often contradictory interpretations? A dialogical methodology remains open to multiple possibilities and, therefore, suspends tendencies toward judgments and discrimination.

Dialogical practitioners recognize that differences may produce unresolvable tensions, and that speakers may not mean exactly what hearers think they do. Instead of agreement, harmony, or certainty, dialogians are more concerned with depth of listening, accuracy of expression, and clarity of understanding. Inquirers participate within tensions between theories and methods. Engaging and being engaged requires both an effort to know about a subject-field and the task of awakening a genuine educational relationship as we seek knowledge and understanding together.

A dialogical pedagogy neither claims to possess the truth, nor does it abandon one to relativism and subjectivity. Instead, it encourages teachers and students to differentiate between being right about one's position and being committed to open-minded inquiry.

POINTS TO REMEMBER

Dialogue is a meta-methodology when its practice—turning, listening, addressing, responding—facilitates the integration of contrasting, even conflicting views.

- As a meta-method, dialogue bridges and integrates both the social sciences and the humanities.
- A learning community embodies: diversity, ambiguity, creative conflict, honesty, humility, and freedom.
- The interhuman reality signifies a place (mutuality) and calls for an interaction (dialogue).
- The dialogical method allows conflicting viewpoints to implicate—highlight and challenge—each other.

NOTES

1. William E. Paden, *Interpreting the Sacred: Ways of Viewing Religion* (Boston: Beacon Press, 1992/2003), 1–2, 8–9.

2. Diana Eck, *Encountering God: A Spiritual Journey from Bozeman to Banaras* (Boston: Beacon Press, 1993), 198.

3. Eck, *Encountering God*, 197–98.

4. Parker J. Palmer, *The Courage to Teach: Exploring the Inner Landscape of a Teacher's Life* (San Francisco: Jossey-Bass, 1997), 110–11.

5. Todd Perreira, in an e-mail from February 2007. The quotation from W. C. Smith appears in "Comparative Religion: Whither and Why?" in *The History of Religions: Essays in Methodology*, ed. Mircea Eliade and Joseph M. Kitagawa (Chicago: University of Chicago Press, 1959), 34.

Part II

Application and Practice

Chapter Five

Dialogues with Texts

Much of the material studied in the humanities and social sciences—whether printed or electronic, whether historical or ethnographic, whether sacred or critical—is textual. One of the most important pieces of information on the class syllabus, therefore, is the list of required texts or readings. Yet while studying texts is important for most classes, little attention is paid to the way in which one reads, to how one interacts with the words.

An unspoken assumption seems to underlie the syllabus—namely, that each student reader will benefit more or less equally by reading the written words. Despite the importance of reading skills for academic success, teachers usually take these skills for granted, presupposing that students have already acquired the ability to read in high school or elsewhere in the university. But is this true?

WHY READ?

Before we can address the question of how to read dialogically, we have to address the larger question: Why read in the first place? Students increasingly have less interest in reading texts. They think they can find everything they need to know on Google.[1] The old order may be collapsing and texts may have less relevance to students, but should we as teachers accept this fate? Doesn't a good text bring forth good fruit? If so, isn't the text that bears such fruit worth our time?

Let us look at the situation from the student's perspective. As Russell Hunt writes,

> When you consider how much of a North American student's academic reading material occurs in commercially produced textbooks, and when you con-

sider how little of the actual text in those volumes was generated for any
purpose beyond the delivering of information to students, it becomes easy to
see how seldom students can have had much experience with texts which
actually exhibit the sorts of intellectual and social motives that animate the
text's scholars . . . to read and write in the course of their careers.[2]

Based on his own research into student reading practices, Hunt argues that
students regularly read in an "'information driven' way: focused on remem-
bering what was in the text [for the exam] rather than assembling it into a
picture, a story."[3]

When faced with texts that are not information-driven, therefore, the
question "Why should I have to read this text?" seems, to the student, per-
fectly legitimate. Legitimate or not, the question offers itself up as a perfect
dialogue starter. Rather than letting students register their silent resistance by
not reading, we might open the first day of class by asking them to respond to
the question of why we should, or should not, read at all. Is it important to
read texts? What type? If not, why not?

Come prepared with a few possible answers to introduce in the course of
the discussion:

- It cleans away the dirt and debris of outmoded ideas.
- It provides a vitamin-like stimulation to elevate and inspire consciousness.
- It allows us to exercise our intellectual muscles.
- It enables us to develop our empathic skills by asking us to identify with
  another's viewpoint.
- It provides insights and ideas that shape and reshape one's stand in the
  world: what one thinks, what one feels, what one believes, how one acts,
  and what one says.
- It enhances one's writing, critical thinking, and oral presentation skills.
- It enables us to continually learn from the past by opening doors into
  where humans have traveled, both physically and intellectually, both sci-
  entifically and nonscientifically, both imaginatively and realistically.
- It affords advice on how to be decent, honorable, wise, compassionate,
  and offers a taste of transcendence, a finite slice of the ineffable Other.
- It clarifies one's intention with regard to living a life worthy of certain
  values, certain principles, and certain wisdoms.

After discussing these and a variety of other reasons why it is important to
engage with a text, it is necessary to offer students some guidelines for
reading, not reading simply for information, but for approaching texts in
ways that will maximize the student's ability to understand and interpret
meaning. Thomas C. Foster, a professor of literature at the University of
Michigan says: "A moment occurs in this exchange between professor and

student when each of us adopts a look. My look says, 'What, you don't get it?' Theirs says, 'We don't get it. And we think you're making it up.' We're having a communication problem. Basically, we've all read the same [text], but we haven't used the same analytical apparatus."[4]

HOW TO READ

To address this communication problem, one must make a fundamental distinction between reading for facts, data, and information versus reading for ideas, patterns, and meanings. Another way to put this is to differentiate between a *surface* approach to reading and a *deep* approach to reading. Julian Hermida writes:

> A surface approach to reading is the tacit acceptance of information contained in the text. Students taking a surface approach to reading usually consider this information as isolated and unlinked facts. This leads to superficial retention of material for examinations and does not promote understanding or long-term retention of knowledge and information. In contrast, a deep approach to reading is an approach where the reader uses higher-order cognitive skills such as the ability to analyze, synthesize, solve problems, and thinks meta-cognitively in order to negotiate meanings with the author and to construct new meanings from the text. The deep reader focuses on the author's message, on the ideas she is trying to convey, the line of argument, and the structure of the argument.[5]

This way of expressing fundamentally different approaches to texts bears striking similarities to Buber's two ways of learning: I-It (surface reading) and I-Thou (deep reading).

Buber offers reader-oriented strategies that involve treating a text not as data, not as an object or an It, but as a Thou. But how does one enter into a meaningful dialogue with a text? Buber suggests making the words immediately present, as if hearing the voice of the speaker. He proposes turning with one's whole being toward the speaker, adopting a "saying of Thou" attitude toward the text, and receiving the indivisible wholeness of something spoken. Buber invited readers of *I and Thou* to read texts dialogically and imaginatively.

But how does this way of reading work?

Gillian Silverman, associate professor of English at University of Colorado–Denver, without referring to Buber has depicted Buber's view of texts. Silverman writes that books can become "living friends": "We open a book, or, rather, it 'opens up' to us, not unlike the friend who responds to our sympathetic probing. . . . We don't want to give up our experience of reading as an 'opening' into another mind, as a progressive exploration registered in the turning of pages, of thoughts that originated elsewhere."[6]

BUBER'S PRACTICES

If the I-Thou relationship requires a mutuality that embraces both I and Thou, what is the character of this reciprocity in our relationship with texts? That is, how does one engage in a mutual back-and-forth relationship with words that seem static on the page? In 1957, almost forty years after Buber wrote *I and Thou*, he added a postscript in which he addressed frequently asked questions from students and colleagues about the meaning of his thought. Therein, Buber answers the question of how to enter into dialogue with inanimate texts.

Buber's practices are:

- make the text present as if spoken in your ears,
- turn to the speaker,
- adopt the "Saying of Thou" attitude,
- hear the voices of the speaker, and
- receive the indivisible wholeness of something spoken.

Buber writes that we can enjoin the text in the reciprocal life of dialogue by making it present as a living Thou. To do this, "we must turn with our whole being to the speaker (who is not to hand) to the saying (which is to hand)." If we succeed in this, Buber writes, we "will hear a voice, perhaps only indistinguishably at first" and receive "the indivisible wholeness of something spoken" as if by a genuine master or teacher. [7]

But how does one go about making a text present to oneself as if it is a living Thou?

When a person reads a book as if encountering another person, he or she must be willing to experience the "otherness" of the text as an embodied dialogical partner like oneself. When one says "Thou" to the text, it requires, at the same time, the saying of "I," the mutual confirmation of both voices in the dialogue. In this *mutual confirmation of the self and text*, the reader is brought into a more intense realization of the text's presence. As well, the reader becomes more aware of his or her situation, circumstances, and attitudes.

One way to embody the text as a Thou and allow this mutual confirmation is to *read the text aloud*. The written word is never content to remain frozen on a page. It calls out for dialogue, for a continuing conversation with the reader. In this sense, each text is a "spokenness" addressed personally, uniquely, and specifically to the eyes and ears of the one reading/hearing it. When one receives the language of the text with one's ears, as if being addressed through spoken words, the text comes alive in a way that it cannot when read silently.

To really engage the text, it is necessary to turn with one's whole being toward the speaker/author of the text, so a *shift in orientation* is required. When Buber speaks of "turning," he describes a double movement: (1) *away* from one's preoccupations and identifications with self, with one's own ideas, with one's own needs; and (2) *toward* full relationship with the text as other, the text as Thou, with one's complete attention.

Buber speaks of bringing a "sense of wonder" to the text: "Be sure not to look for anything in particular, but rather enter without any preconceived notions into the realm the book opens before you. Let it astonish you. Do not let yourself be irritated if its manner differs from what you are accustomed to, or even what you consider correct."[8] This act of turning—away from one's preoccupations and biases—allows room for the astonishment of genuine dialogue.

When reading dialogically, one *hears* the addressing voice, recognizes who is speaking, and then can respond directly and honestly to the text from where one stands. The practice of *reading slowly and more mindfully* is like becoming acquainted with another person. It's like having a genuine dialogue with a friend in which each person is reinvigorated.

No longer treating the text as an object, no longer separating it into content and style, no longer reducing it to the content of one's own experience, one is addressed by the individual wholeness of something spoken.

And finally, one should *respond responsibly* to this voice of the text. The dialogue remains incomplete until the reader/hearer brings his or her interpretation into the public realm of the between. This requires a second turning, one away from the reader/hearer's own individual experience of dialogue out into the shared dialogue of the communal—in this case, classroom—space. As A. David Moody urges his students:

> Ignore the jungle of criticism (including my own contribution to it) and concentrate on articulating the way in which the poetry articulates you. They [the students] do not believe me, of course. I can't mean it, since I am a teacher—it must be a trick to keep them from mastering my mystery. . . . They have been educated to suppress their own experience and their gropings for the meaning of it and to go in instead for "scholarly research." . . . The sad consequence is that good students become able to discuss the meaning of a poem without its necessarily meaning anything at all to them.[9]

CONDITIONED INTERPRETATION

When employing a dialogical approach to texts, the nature of our inquiry is an interactive one occurring between a living text (in which one can hear the author's voice) and a reader who is vitally interested in understanding and applying its meaning. In thus engaging and being engaged, one makes the words immediately present, as if hearing the voice of the author, and turns with one's whole being toward the speaker with a receptive attitude.

The invigorating renewal of this approach to texts transforms both text and reader/hearer because, as the Russian literary critic Mikhail Bakhtin writes, "There is neither a first nor a last word and there are no limits to the dialogical context (it extends into the boundless past and the boundless future)."[10] Even so, we are all conditioned by our training, background, and biases. Buber writes:

> I know that no interpretation, including my own, coincides with the original meaning of the text. I know that my interpreting, like everyone else's, is conditioned through my being. But if I attend as faithfully as I can to what it contains of word and texture, of sound and rhythmic structure, of open and hidden connections, my interpretation will not have been made in vain—I find something, I have found something.[11]

Buber continues, "I make visible the working forces of the text that I have experienced."[12] What is crucial is to remain as faithful as one can to the words that are there—not to possess their truth, but to share them in the common discourse.

DIALOGICAL LENS

Reading through a dialogical lens, one discovers and responds to the links between personal life and textual insights. The act of reading takes place in a conversational field and involves reciprocal and reciprocating interactions between author and text, author and reader, and reader and text. Entering into real dialogues with the text necessitates both applying the text's message to the reader's life and sharing the resulting interpretation with a community of inquiry.

Through a dialogical lens, readers discover and respond to links between their personal lives and the textual insights that engage them. The activity of reading takes place on a conversational field and involves interplay between author and text, author and reader, and reader and text. A text, as visualized in figure 1, is not just a soliloquy or monologue, nor is any one interpretation merely subjective. Rather, a fruitful reciprocity exists between the reader, the author/text, and other interpretive voices, with dialogue at the center.[13]

INTERTEXTUAL DIALOGUES

What happens when one places two or more texts side by side in the mind and allows the voice of one to speak and respond to the voice of the other? There are at least four intertextual relations at play when we begin reading

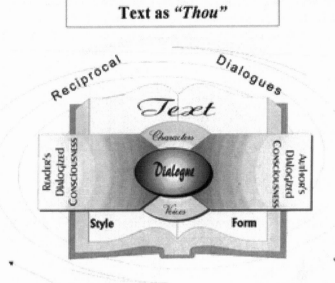

Figure 1

dialogically *and* intertextually: (1) the relations between an author's quotes in her single text; (2) the relations between the author's previous texts and her current text; (3) the relations between the selected text and other cognate (i.e., similar) texts; and (4) the relations between subsequent readings of one text, which will inevitably be influenced by other texts.

In these intertextual relationships, two or more texts meet and dialogue within the reader's imagination (Buber's "imagining the real"). Each text is reanimated by its dialogue with the other and made more available to interpretation and understanding. This process involves placing two different texts side by side, reading them in each other's light, and, in that associative framework, discovering a revitalized understanding of the one through the other and vice versa.

An example would be to bring Martin Buber's "Elements of the Interhuman" into dialogue with Shin'ichi Hisamatsu's "Characteristics of Oriental Nothingness."[14] Does juxtaposing the thought of Buber and Hisamatsu—one Western, one Eastern; one Jewish, one Buddhist; one German-speaking, one Japanese-speaking; one pointing to God, one pointing to True Self—seem plausible? It may not, until we recognize that Buber's "Between," can meaningfully interact with Hisamatsu's "Oriental Nothingness."

If we place these writers in dialogue with one another, each author's subject can be more deeply understood. In "Elements of the Interhuman,"

Buber clarified his philosophy of dialogue as expressed in previous works. Buber focused specifically on his concept of the "Between." In "Characteristics of the Oriental Nothingness," Hisamatsu focused on the theme of "Nothingness." Hisamatsu presented concisely what he believed "Nothingness" *was not*—along with six positive characteristics of what it is.

What emerges as common between these two essays is that both the "Between" and "Nothingness" can only be manifest when one is spontaneously, unself-consciously present in the here-and-now. Being present, responding freely and creatively, without withholding, without distractions, without evaluating, without comparing and judging, is being responsibly responsive to whomever or whatever presents itself.

POINTS TO REMEMBER

Dialogues with texts occur only to the extent that the text is engaged as a Thou, as a voice that invites response, rather than as an It, as frozen words on a page.

- Reading a text as a Thou challenges readers to engage it personally.
- Four necessary attitudes are required of a reader: receptivity, suspension of bias, reflection, and application.
- By reacting to the voice of a text, the reader clarifies his or her stance.
- Reading a text as an It allows one to objectify its ideas and critically analyze them.
- Intertextual dialogues allow texts to interpret and reinvigorate each other.

NOTES

1. A. B. Credaro says that while "there are over four billion unique publically accessible websites . . . only 6% of these have educational content," and that while "anyone can publish a webpage—no one checks that the information is correct." A. B. Credaro, "Research Findings: The Relationship between School Libraries and Academic Achievement," *Principal Matters* 53 (November 2002): 35–36.

2. Russell A. Hunt, "Reading and Writing for Real: Why It Matters for Learning," *Atlantic Universities' Teaching Showcase* 55: 137.

3. Hunt, "Reading and Writing for Real."

4. Thomas C. Foster, *How to Read Literature like a Professor* (New York: Harper, 2003), xiii.

5. Julian Hermida, "The Importance of Teaching Academic Reading Skills in First-Year University Courses," *The International Journal of Research and Review* 3 (September 2009): 21.

6. Gillian Silverman, "It's Alive!" *New York Times Book Review*, August 12, 2012, 31.

7. Martin Buber, *I and Thou*, 128.

8. Martin Buber, "Advice to Frequenters of Libraries," Books for Your Vacation, *Branch Library Book News* (The New York Public Library) 21, no. 5 (1944): 81–82.

9. A. David Moody, *Thomas Stearns Eliot: Poet* (Cambridge: Cambridge University Press, 1979), 137–38.

10. Mikhail Bakhtin, *Speech Genres and Other Late Essays*, trans. Vern McGee (Austin: University of Texas Press, 1986), 170. Bakhtin continues: "At any moment in the development of the dialogue there are immense, boundless masses of forgotten contextual meanings, but at certain moments of the dialogue's subsequent development along the way they are recalled and invigorated in renewed form (in a new context). Nothing is absolutely dead: every meaning will have its homecoming festival."

11. Martin Buber, *Pointing the Way*, trans. Maurice Friedman (New York: Schocken Books, 1991), 100.

12. Buber, *Pointing the Way*, 100.

13. For a fuller explanation of interpreting texts dialogically, see Stephen Kepnes, *The Text as Thou: Martin Buber's Dialogical Hermeneutics and Narrative Theology* (Bloomington: Indiana University Press, 1992), especially part I.

14. The following paragraphs appear in a longer essay: Kenneth Kramer, "Cross-Reanimating Martin Buber's 'Between' and Shin'ichi Hisamatsu's 'Nothingness,'" *Journal of Ecumenical Studies* 46, no. 3 (Summer 2011).

Chapter Six

Dialogues with Students

Now that students can go online to access brilliant lectures in various fields, it is logical to ask: can the complete contents of a university course be commoditized by technology? Richard A. DeMillo, author of *Abelard to Apple: The Fate of American Colleges and Universities*, for one, doesn't think so. DeMillo speaks of a student's need to experience passing through a network of teachers. Discussing iTunes U in particular, he argues, "What you get there is pretty much all you need to get students involved in discussion. But that's not the discussion. The discussion is what takes place afterward, maybe not in the classroom, but in the learning community. That's where professors can add value."[1]

Important discussions—the kinds that bring education to life—occur preeminently in interactive classes. Many times, students' questions in response to the material will lead to further questions and to a deepening of both the teacher's and students' understanding of a subject. Only in the physical classroom do invaluable exchanges spontaneously occur. The unpredictable responses found in the classroom contain new insights.

THE FLIGHT FROM DIALOGUE

On the front page of the April 22, 2012, *New York Times'* Sunday Review, twelve people show the numerous ways one can use a phone while remaining oblivious to his or her surroundings.[2] Its author, psychologist Sherry Turkle, suggests that while we are constantly communicating in a technological universe, we've substituted connection for conversation. In our digital culture, we have become tethered to a screen that's always on and that connects us, through a variety of genres, to a global consciousness. Students, if they can, receive e-mails, send texts, and post on Facebook during classes. Technology-enabled, we've become accustomed to a new way of being—"alone together."[3]

E-mail, Twitter, texting, and posting (just to name a few) force us to only be partially present in any given moment. Turkle suggests that these forms of connection allow us to "present the self we want to be. This means we can edit. And if we wish to, we can delete. Or retouch: the voice, the flesh, the face, the body. Not too much, not too little—just right. Human relationships are rich; they're messy and demanding. We have learned the habit of cleaning them up with technology."[4] Elsewhere she writes:

> Face-to-face conversation unfolds slowly. It teaches patience. When we communicate on our digital devices, we learn different habits. As we ramp up the volume and velocity of online connections, we start to expect faster answers. To get these, we ask one another simpler questions; we dumb down our communications, even on the most important matters. It is as though we have all put ourselves on cable news. Shakespeare might have said, "we are consum'd with that which we were nourish'd by."[5]

For Buber, the flight from genuine dialogue has a deeper cause—it occurs whenever we fail to turn away from our own self-preoccupations (whatever they are, however they are enacted) and wholeheartedly toward the other. Instead of turning toward the other, dialogue is prevented by the act of reflexion—bending back upon oneself. Dialogue cannot happen when I choose to remain a self-contained individual, when I refuse to stop what I am doing, and when I am *unaware* of an invitation to become We.

BECOMING WE

By contrast, dialogue, whether spoken or silent, becomes genuine (real, authentic) when:

- it is mutual, two-sided, reciprocally experienced;
- it is unreserved, without judging, without withholding, with nothing left out;
- it occurs in the Between, a sphere which is common to each person, but which reaches out beyond the special domain of each;
- it embodies reciprocal and reciprocating wholeness (unity of body, mind, spirit) between each person; and
- it expresses the action and passion, speaking and listening of one person intertwined with the action and passion, listening and speaking of the another—challenging, questioning, reinforcing, reshaping each other's stand.

Lauren, a junior at the University of California–Santa Cruz who is double majoring in cognitive science and psychology, like other college students today and those younger, has grown up understanding and using the latest technological tools. A question was posed by one of her teachers: "Do you think that friends, or family members, or perhaps even strangers, who put themselves fully and attentively into their electronic interactions with another, and who then respond fully and honestly and without withholding anything from another, could be said to be entering into a genuine dialogue with that person? After all, the technology is, in and of itself, neutral."

Lauren responded: "It's interesting just how heated people become when discussing communication technology. They recognize the influence that others have on neutral social media, yet continually fail to recognize their own role in making it a tool for positive change or the opposite. Does this mean that we really are losing our ability to effectively communicate if people are losing their awareness of the influence that we have on each other?"

"Can it be assumed," the teacher responded, "that based on your remarks it is possible to engage in a genuine conversation digitally?"

"I think it's possible, but not for me. I am a person who constantly wonders if my message is being interpreted as I intend and textual communication often goes awry. Although I find it a very personal media, words on a page can't be read with the emphasis with which I type them."

Encounters such as this one, in which questions generate further questions, and in which the student's response redirects the teacher's as well as the teacher's response redirecting the student's, bring each student and teacher to the immediacy of the educative process. In a sense, by becoming open to the other's perspective, each becomes a resource for the other.

AS DIALOGUE

Martin Buber, even though he lectured in a Germanic manner, made sure that he opened up a space for students' questions and discussion. Maurice Friedman writes that in Buber's first visit to America, "he was very much like a formal professor from Germany, but after his lectures, he always made a point to speak person-to-person. After a lecture at Yale University, Buber spoke for twenty minutes with a woman who had asked him a question from the audience. Years later, she spoke of how much this dialogical intimacy had meant and still meant to her."[6]

Dialogues with students are, at their best, always unique to the student's situation as he or she presents it. Some students require intellectual stimulation and guidance; others need encouragement with their life circumstances. Some seek curricular resources; others, extracurricular applications of the course material. Some need assistance in developing critical understanding; others seek guidance for enhancing their interpretations and applications of the course material.

Todd Perreira once described the value of this dialogical approach to teaching in the following way: "I was flabbergasted one day when Kramer asked me to teach the first ten minutes of his class to explain my point of view on a text and then urged me to go on for another ten minutes because he was so enjoying my lecture!"[7]

Teaching isn't about the teacher. It's about the process. Teachers looking for refreshing bite-sized wisdom should remember: Trust the dialogical process itself.

James Brown, a former student and new teacher, called and said,

> I want to thank you for something you said a while ago. You said that teaching isn't about the teacher, so I made my teaching primarily about interacting with students. Things changed for sure. That really made all the difference during the semester. Afterwards students gave me great reviews, which I hadn't anticipated at the start. A psychologist, who wants to be a lawyer and who is struggling with anger-management, came up to me and thanked me for showing him "a better way." He was referring, of course, to the way of dialogue.

TRUSTING

At times teaching can be a performance art in that unexpected and entertaining surprises become part of the process. In the words of Queen's "Bohemian Rhapsody":

> Is this the real life?
> Is this just fantasy?
> Caught in a landslide,
> No escape from reality.
> Open your eyes,
> Look up to the skies and see,
> I'm just a poor boy, I need no sympathy,
> Because I'm easy come, easy go,
> Little high, little low,
> Any way the wind blows doesn't really matter to
> me, to me.[8]

In an academic context, we tend to get caught in a landslide of habitual behaviors, attitudes, opinions, beliefs, judgments that prevent us from really seeing. These lyrics ask us to temporarily bracket our assumptions and opinions, to put them aside for the class period so that we can really *open* our eyes and look out to what is encountered with an open mind.

If the beginning of dialogue involves turning toward the other, "turning" itself is made possible by trusting. Whenever we enter into relationships we risk becoming wounded, and we have built up an arsenal of defenses against this danger. Understandably, we fear emotional pain. Therefore, becoming open to being wounded by the other absolutely requires trusting the other. It also involves trusting in the possibility and power of dialogue itself, and in our personal ability to handle emotional pain, whenever it arises.

Existential trust through a Buberian lens points to:

- willingness to live from moment to moment and to meet what each new moment brings;
- accepting the fact that a genuine relationship is two-sided and therefore beyond the control of our will;
- having the courage to address and the courage to respond;
- openness and willingness to listen to the other.[9]

How can one develop trust? This question is both dangerous and fruitful. The question is dangerous if it traps you in the exploration of strategies or practices or techniques within yourself. The question if fruitful if it leads you back into real relationship.

Here's the point: trust isn't one-sided. It builds through reciprocal and reciprocated passions, ideas, feelings, and instincts between persons in genuine relationship. As Mechthild Gawlick, a graduate student in anthropology, says, "When you fully throw yourself into relationship, at times you are confirmed, but at times you are hurt. Trust can develop only by trusting."

TEN PEDAGOGICAL TOOLS

A highly motivated student, who wanted to become a teacher, was invited by her professor to be attentive to *how* her teachers taught, and then to compile a list of pedagogical strategies that she felt were successful. At the end of the semester, she presented a list based on her experience in her classes. Together, with her professor, the following list was shaped:

1. *Repetition*—Asking a student to repeat what you have just said in their own language to a student who has arrived late.
2. *Fearlessness*—Being unafraid to practice the fine art of self-deprecation; being willing to speak irreverently about yourself.
3. *Humor*—Using spontaneous humor at any and all times.
4. *Timing*—Knowing when to retrieve people's attention with a sudden shift of direction; peppering the presentation with attention-grabbing comments.
5. *Inviting*—Couching directives in the form of invitations.

6. *Sensitivity*—Being sensitive to the individual student's situation so that you can spontaneously apply/tailor the material to the student's intellectual needs.

7. *Translating*—Being ready to translate any occasion into an example of what you are trying to communicate.

8. *Segueing*—Learning the inestimable value of segueing from one thought/idea into another, no matter how far it seems to be removed from the former, to illustrate a point.

9. *Openness*—Remaining wholeheartedly open to suggestions that come from students even if they seem to contradict the teacher's agenda.

10. *Spontaneity*—Leaving room for pedagogical ploys that have not yet announced themselves so that there is always room for the as-of-yet-undisclosed teaching tool to emerge spontaneously.

For a dialogical pedagogy to really work, it cannot finally be planned out ahead of time. Yes, you can plan it to the extent that you designate a class, or a portion of a class, for give-and-take exchange between student and teacher. Yes, you can plan it to the extent that you can ask students to come prepared to enter into a dialogue with you. Yet, the actual engagement itself is always original, always unique, and always contains content that could not have been pre-planned.

TAKING RISKS

While not every class should be conducted in this manner—depending on the size of the class, the subject matter studied, and the timing during the semester—it is always appropriate to designate time, especially in smaller classes of twenty to thirty students, for teacher-student dialogues. There are several kinds of in-class dialogues including small group dialogues and teacher-student dialogues. More important than the form of the dialogues themselves, however, is the spirit of risk-taking behind them. [10]

Before one enters a dialogue, consider what conditions have to be met. Curiosity is the force that drives the questioner. If you don't have curiosity—genuine curiosity coming up from the center of your being—the question may not be worth much. But, along with curiosity, it is important to have some sense of the person whom you are addressing. You have to have some sense of how that person is grounded, that is, their training and education and inspiration.

But there is one condition that matters most, that is: in every dialogue there are how many voices? Three: the third voice is the voice of the dialogue itself, the voice of the dialogical relationship. Dialogue is not limited to the conversers; it is born from the dialogical interaction itself.

Indeed, to teach dialogically, it is essential to trust the process; this trust expands the more one is able to set one's notes for the class to the side and face the students with a willing openness to enter into a living exchange with them about the assigned material. When it is genuine, dialogue cannot be pre-planned or predicted. Real dialogical encounters present their own circumstances. Real dialogue is spontaneous; it is two-sided; it is always unique to the situation, to the participants. A dialogical encounter calls forth from each person a "common *logos*," a mutually shared speech-with-meaning.

STUDENT AND TEACHER REVIEWS

Throughout the semester, it is useful to elicit students' responses to the course as they have experienced it so far. Periodic reviews are better than end-of-semester reviews because they promote dialogue within the class before it's too late to adjust one's approach. One way to elicit student feedback is to present students with the following questions.

1. What's missing from our class discussions that would clarify the topic at hand?
2. How would I [i.e., the student] present this material?
3. What new questions are generated by our understandings and interpretations?

Another way to elicit student's responses is to respond to their class contributions, especially with regard to the impact they have on the teacher. By acknowledging the significance of students' specific remarks and how they expand the teacher's own views, the students not only feel heard, but are much more likely to continue participating.

QUESTIONING THE QUESTIONER

Dialogical learning takes the form of question and answer. Asking good questions is an invaluable pedagogical tool. A dialogical teacher does not just give answers, but also shares his or her own questions with students. Let students know that asking questions, rather than a sign of weakness as some of them may think, is a sign of curiosity, of interest, and of a desire to learn. Maurice Friedman writes:

> Once after an incredibly strenuous and exhausting two days as visiting lecturer at a college, I recalled Buber's statement to me, "I wish people would ask me more real questions," and I understood it with a depth I had never previously attained. Buber was not saying that he was a fount of knowledge, but that if

persons approached him with *real* questions, then something would come into
being between him and them that would not otherwise have arisen. [11]

It was also important, for Buber, that the teacher should ask students genuine
questions "to which he does not know the full answer himself and the student
in turn should give the teacher information concerning his experiences and
opinions. Conversely, when the teacher is asked a question by the student, his
reply should proceed from the depths of his own personal experience." [12]

It is equally important to respond to a student's question by repeating the
same question to the person who asked it. Not always, certainly, and never
cavalierly. This sounds like "active listening," and is, but it is active listening
directed toward dialogical outcomes, not toward understanding in order to
rebut.

Parker J. Palmer says, "Attentive listening is never an easy task—it con-
sumes psychic energy at a rate that tires and surprises me. But it is made
easier when I am holding back my own authoritative impulses. When I
suspend, for just a while, my inner chatter about what I am going to say next,
I open room within myself to receive the external conversation." [13]

Depending on the questioner's situation, circumstances, and investment
in the question, it is at times helpful to rephrase the question for the student
and reach for the connection he or she is trying to make underneath it. By
asking students to first respond to their own questions, the teacher may be
better able to respond in a way that both affirms views and challenge them
with an expanded perspective.

POINTS TO REMEMBER

Dialogue with students, when reciprocal, is a force that drives the address-
response educational process.

• When one cannot step outside of self-preoccupations, one misses another's invitation to engage in dialogue.
• A dialogical approach to education always opens up time for questions
  and discussion.
• Entering into genuine dialogue requires one to turn away from self and
  fully toward the other.
• Ten pedagogical tools are: repetition, fearlessness, humor, timing, inviting, sensitivity, translating, segueing, openness, spontaneity.
• For dialogue to become genuine, one must risk not knowing ahead of time
  what will be said.

NOTES

1. Richard DeMillo, "The Future Can't Wait," *New York Times*, November 6, 2011, 31.

2. Sherry Turkle, "The Flight from Conversation," Sunday Review, *New York Times*, April 22, 2012, 6–8.

3. See Sherry Turkle, *Alone Together: Why We Expect More from Technology and Less from Each Other* (New York: Basic Books, 2011). Turkle writes: "The narrative of *Alone Together* describes an arc: we expect more from technology and less from each other. . . . Overwhelmed, we have been drawn to connections that seem low risk and always at hand: Facebook friends, avatars, IRC chat partners." She proposes that we may need to reclaim good manners by talking face-to-face without cell phones at hand, and to look "toward the virtues of solitude, deliberateness, and living fully in the moment" (295–96).

4. Turkle, "The Flight from Conversation," 6.

5. Turkle, "The Flight from Conversation," 6. MIT President Rafael Reif suggests that higher education is developing between attaining a brick-and-mortar, face-to-face "degree" or an internet classrooms and laboratories "certificate" or "credential." See Thomas Friedman, "Revolution Hits the Universities," *New York Times*, January 27, 2013, 11.

6. Maurice Friedman, *My Friendship with Martin Buber* (New York: Syracuse University Press, 2013), chapter 4.

7. Todd Perreira, in a January 25, 1995, letter to the Outstanding Professor Committee at San José State University.

8. Freddie Mercury, "Bohemian Rhapsody," EMI, 1975.

9. Maurice Friedman, *Touchstones of Reality: Existential Trust and the Community of Peace* (New York: E. P. Dutton, 1972), 318–31.

10. See Parker J. Palmer, *The Courage to Teach: Exploring the Inner Landscape of a Teacher's Life* (San Francisco, Jossey-Bass, 1997). Parker writes: "We can educate the heart by exposing it to tension-inducing ideas, relationships, and experiences—expose it in situations where we can reflect together and mentor each other on how best to hold these tensions, and on what happens within us and around us when we do not hold them well." Interview with Parker Palmer: Tension, Heartbreak, and Vocation, *Reflections* 99, no. 1 (Spring 2012): 68.

11. Maurice Friedman, *A Dialogue with Hasidic Tales: Hallowing the Everyday* (New York: Insight Books, 1988), 76. Friedman continues: "As Buber stressed at the outset, the ultimate purpose of teaching is to enable the learner to find his or her own ground" (83).

12. Martin Buber, "A New Venture in Adult Education," *The Hebrew University of Jerusalem*, Semi-Jubilee Volume (Jerusalem: The Hebrew University, April 1950), 117. Buber's remarks are quoted in Maurice Friedman, *Martin Buber: The Life of Dialogue* (Chicago: The University of Chicago Press, 1955), 183.

13. Palmer, *The Courage to Teach*, 138. Palmer writes: "Some questions close down the space and keep students from thinking: 'What did the textbook have to say about concepts. . . .' Other questions open up so much space that they lose students in a trackless wasteland. The questions that help people learn are found somewhere between these extremes: 'If you had been one of these researchers, how would you have decided what race your subjects were?'" (136–37).

Chapter Seven

Interview Dialogues

Across many academic fields, including education, there exists a pervasive human-relational difficulty; one that drives a seemingly impenetrable wedge between persons—namely, the lack of real dialogue. Unfortunately, very few who use the word take the time to understand what it involves and even fewer have spent time developing the sensitivity and skill necessary to practice it.

What is needed, especially in educational contexts, is a workable practice of genuine dialogue that truly considers every person in his or her particular situation. Real dialogue offers such a solution. The point of view that has been advanced here is deliberately evocative: only real dialogue leads toward overcoming the self-contained and self-deceiving naïveté of monological points of view. This is because mutual dialogue is three-voiced. It includes the voice of the one who speaks, the voice of the one who responds, and the voice of the dialogical relationship itself.

THE PRACTICE OF INTERVIEW DIALOGUES

Although genuine dialogue cannot be reduced to a technique, it can be practiced. This chapter discusses the interview dialogue, an approach to practicing genuine dialogue that can be used in the classroom and in interviews with experts. This practice involves two skills: discernment listening and interactive questioning. They clarify one's intention to engage others dialogically. If genuine dialogue emerges from these techniques, it emerges as a third voice of its own, irreducible to the techniques themselves.

Interview dialogues are more than just structures for a discussion. The discussion itself and the means—discernment listening and interactive questioning—are not of themselves the dialogue, or even the practice of dialogue.

As was indicated in the first chapter, genuine dialogue requires four attitudes. These attitudes constitute the practice of dialogue:

1. *turning* wholly away from self-absorption by giving yourself to relationship and toward encountering the unique other as a dialogical partner;
2. *addressing,* accepting, and valuing this person's expressed stand and making the other person present as your dialogical partner;
3. *listening* attentively, with your whole heart, to what is said/not said and imagining what the other is thinking/feeling/experiencing; and
4. *responding* responsibly and honestly without agenda or withholding yourself and confirming, even when disagreeing, a willingness for future dialogues.

As long as the methods and strategies for facilitating it are not confused with the actual practice itself, interview dialogues create a forum for modeling and facilitating genuine dialogical encounters.

INTERVIEWING EXPERTLY

Enter interviews intending to ask innovative questions, questions that will open up new insights into your conversation partner's view and the subject at hand. Seek answers that open new ways of envisioning what's possible for both parties in the conversation rather than ones that close off creative possibilities and enforce prior opinions. What forms is a result of the unique dynamic between the person being interviewed and oneself.

In practice, students and teachers need to be willing, after asking preplanned questions, to allow the dialogical exchange between themselves and the interviewee to direct further questions. The most important function of the interviewer is to make the interviewee feel comfortable, feel important, and feel listened to. This method has several guiding principles:

1. Secure written permission from the subject to record your interview and then submit it to your professor.
2. Agree on time/place/length of the interview.
3. Prepare several questions ahead of time to ask the interviewee, questions that touch upon course issues but that are open ended.
4. Secure a method for recording the interview.
5. Transcribe the interview.
6. Give a copy of the interview transcription to the interviewee for his or her changes/corrections.

7. Reread and reflect on the transcript, asking yourself what is most important in the interview and what most challenged you.

DISCERNMENT LISTENING

In the interview-dialogue, interviewers should not only listen keenly to what is being said, but also to what is underneath what is said. Different from ordinary listening, in which one assesses, associates, judges, or waits to give one's own point of view, this practice of discernment listening pays attention to what is said within, beneath, and behind spoken words. One attempts to hear what is said on the level of the words, the personal and human experience that informs them.

One afternoon, after a dialogical seminar, a young student from the philosophy department asked two questions that significantly challenged the context of the seminar: "What does Buber say about how I should enter into relationships? Should I prepare for dialogue in a certain way? In other words, can one do something before entering dialogue?"

Turning is the basic movement that initiates dialogical education—the re-orienting of one's body, mind, and spirit toward meaningful relationships with others in the classroom. This includes being fully present, accepting and affirming the other's presence, listening attentively to what is said, and responding honestly.

The central roadblock to turning is reflexion—bending back on oneself. This backward-bending movement privileges self-consciousness and withdrawal from entering into relationships with others. By reducing the other to the content of one's experience, the heart and soul of what is most important begins to get lost.

Genuinely listening to the other cannot occur without turning with one's full attention. Often listening is thought of as "active listening," the prescribed encouragement of maximum levels of feedback. But this form of listening is not necessarily the most effective, especially when it devolves into an exercise in strategy. It could even harm the listening process by fragmenting the listener's attention. Discernment listening means being willing to "hear" the emotional and personal context that gives the ideas a speaker is speaking their unique situation.

INTERACTIVE QUESTIONING

One should, in turn, ask questions that aim toward getting at this closer kind of listening. The practice of discernment listening, therefore, implies the practice of interactive questioning, and vice versa. Different from ordinary questioning, which is single-purposed and designed to ascertain one unambiguous response, interactive questioning allows for co-creative and more personal responses.

Two kinds of questions will help deepen the level of interviewing. The first question is, "What is underneath that?" or "Where do you think that came from?" The purpose is to help the other person become clearer about his or her own story. Buber would say that these questions need to be asked with consideration to avoid sounding arbitrary.

The second question is "What's missing?" What is missing that would clarify this person's response? What is the unsaid thing that would complete this person's story or idea? When one encounters another, whether in the artificial setting of an interview or in daily interactions, asking this question of the other, often silently, reminds one that there is always more passion, more emotion, more personal striving and human experience that shape the person but that words can't express often.

What's behind these questions is the drive for creativity, the desire to co-create this one particular moment between conversational partners. Behind any dialogical method, Buber reminds us, is the desire for continual emergence. The partners are meant to find what's new, what's fresh, what's underneath, what hasn't been noticed. Bringing this spirit into the dialogical encounter allows for freedom within the structure of the interview. It intensifies the moment, like the constrained/spontaneous structure of live jazz.

SELF-DISCOVERIES

When one interviews another person dialogically, one takes a risk, as one does in all true dialogue. Not being certain ahead of time of what you will ask is daunting when one has arranged a formal interview. In fact, however, not planning anything more than two questions—"What's underneath that?" and "What's missing?"—is practice for genuine dialogue in everyday life.

Most of our genuine encounters happen because they are completely unexpected. Maybe no question will show up or the question that does show up will be a mundane, uninteresting, and unimaginative one. The element of risk in dialogue is softened, however, by the fact that one has put oneself in the dialogical situation in the first place. Genuine dialogue leads to self-discoveries.

The final and most important part of the interview is for students and teachers alike to afterward locate their emergent selves in the dialogical encounter. In other words, what have they learned? What has the other taught them about themselves that they could have learned nowhere else?

Mikhail Bakhtin spoke about the fact that we are living lives as people-yet-to-be. Individuals can only experience their yet-to-be-ness in those moments of creativity when something new encounters them. As a teacher and as an interviewer there is an unspoken agenda in the classroom, which is: let the classroom become part of the process of self-discovery. The "I" behind all of this is the "I" over the weekend who reflects back on what has happened during the week and reflects ahead on what is going to be done.

INTERCULTURAL DIALOGUE

Increasingly, classrooms are filled with students and teachers from different cultural backgrounds and holding different educational views. It can be confusing to drift in and out of several different identities. This configuration both challenges clear communication and provides opportunities for enhanced learning. Yet, teachers and students wonder: How can we understand each other and the course material when we're not in agreement?

If a genuine intercultural exchange is to be achieved, one must shift the basis of the encounter from *having* a dialogue (in which two or more people are speaking at each other) to *being* a dialogue (in which two or more people are speaking with each other).

Leonard Swidler writes: "In dialogue I talk with you primarily so that *I* can learn what I cannot perceive from my place in the world, with my personal lenses of knowing. Through your eyes I see what I cannot see from my side of the globe, and *vice versa*. Hence, dialogue is not just a way to gain more information but a whole new way of thinking."[1] Along these lines, he created ten guidelines for participation in constructive intercultural dialogue:

1. Be willing to learn, to grow, and to participate in change.
2. Dialogue is needed both among differing groups and within the same group.
3. Practice honesty and sincerity.
4. Start dialogue with points where agreement is easier.
5. Compare and contrast similar elements of differing traditions.
6. Identify oneself so that someone could speak for you with understanding.
7. Learn how to listen with an open mind without projecting oneself into what "the other" is saying.
8. Level the playing field; as far as possible counter unequal power relations.
9. Risk self-critical thinking on behalf of increasing knowledge.
10. Practice empathy.[2]

But what does one have the right to expect when entering a dialogical encounter? Swidler addresses this question in his "Stages of Transformation" that result from intercultural exchanges. Each participant can expect that meaningful challenges will be posed and addressed, that old ideas will be reshaped, and that transformative directives will emerge. Genuine academic dialogue evokes vital reciprocity because it is in the classroom where persons, in their cultural, ideological, socio-political, and religious particularity, meet and address themselves by addressing the subject at hand.

Several of Swidler's stages—making conscious choices (to engage and not to withdraw), passing over to the other's side (opening in acts of dialogue), and the dialogic awakening (moments of mutual empathy and understanding)—help us realize how each participant's understanding can be broadened and deepened. "Moments of insight that repeat or spiral into new thinking or more enhanced versions of old thinking replace stages of linear development."[3]

HOW TO ENGAGE?

What makes the interview dialogue difficult? How does one overcome this? What can I do as an interviewer to prompt this spontaneous dialogue from the other?

According to Martin Buber, unlike monologue disguised as dialogue, real dialogue occurs only when two or more unique persons converse in an I-Thou structure of honest openness and mutuality in which each person turns completely to the other and responds openly, honestly, and spontaneously to what is said (or left unsaid). In various places, Buber uses words such as *genuine* or *authentic* or *true* or *real* with the word *dialogue* to point beyond what is ordinarily meant by the term (i.e., having a dialogue) to a more participatory exchange (i.e., being a dialogue).

Buber was well aware that each person is encased in a metaphorical "armor" that impedes dialogue and therefore makes genuine dialogue an infrequent occurrence. Nevertheless, he was motivated to break through the armor of apathy, habitual behavior, and monologue into a genuine interaction between persons.

But how?

The first and last step is to turn with full listening attention toward the other. The act of turning with all of one's energy is necessary to initiate and sustain the dialogical flow. When one is really interested in what the other says—not as the content of one's own experience, but as an opening for transformational growth—mutually enriching educational exchanges occur.

This applies, as well, to the student-teacher relationship. We all like to talk about ourselves, but when someone really listens to what we are saying, our interest in the dialogue itself intensifies.

WHAT'S MISSING?

What's missing from this chapter is concrete examples. The following are responses that Elisabeth Kübler-Ross, Ram Dass, and Brother David Steindl-Rast provided in interviews conducted in a Death, Dying, and Religions class. How would one explain similarities and differences in the approaches and understanding of the question: What's missing?

Elisabeth Kübler-Ross

The Swiss-born psychiatrist was the first professional in the field to really listen to the voice of dying patients and to give them a public forum. Her five stages of responding to death and dying—denial, anger, bargaining, depression, and acceptance—have become universally known. [4]

Kramer: The first question I would like to ask you, Elisabeth, is a question that I have asked each of the people that I have interviewed: What do you think is the missing element in the way that people respond to death and dying, the lack of which keeps them from having a healthier attitude toward death?

Ross: They have no evolved spiritual problem. If they have any spiritual sense, they are in touch throughout the living world with their soul. They will know that dying is nothing to be afraid of. They are afraid to look inside, they are afraid to look to what God is all about. They don't know anything about human evolution. They worry about taxes, making a living, getting through the year, or a tax year, or whatever, and they don't go beyond that. They are like in kindergarten. And then those human beings who are in kindergarten should not worry about those things, because they are not there yet. That's where evolution takes place. When they finally begin to worry about it, they get excited, [. . .] and then their spiritual quadrant opens and then they ask the right question and then they get the answer. You just have to ask and you find out. But you have to be at a certain level of evolution to even consider that.

Ram Dass

Ram Dass, also known as Richard Alpert, is a professor of psychology as well as the author of the highly influential book *Be Here Now*. In it, he takes readers on a journey into the heart of Hindu spirituality and addresses the importance of being fully present in each moment. [5]

Kramer: What do you think is missing from most ordinary conversations about death and dying? And by that I mean: What's missing, say, the presence of which would enable human beings to be more creative in the face of death?

Ram Dass: What's usually missing from dealing with death and dying in our culture is that we take our separateness seriously, as absolute reality. We really think we're "somebody." And if you're somebody, you're absolutely going to die. We don't recognize the other planes of consciousness in which we aren't separate entities. There are equally real planes in which we are simply awareness, which has nothing to do with birth and death. Births come and deaths come, and on it goes, and insofar as "awareness" is concerned, you are still right here.

With birth and early childhood, you go into "somebody" training; then you start taking yourself seriously; and you cultivate your somebodyness, and go to San José State and become somebody special. And then, with grace, you start awakening, and realize, "God, did I get trapped in that dream!" And you start to wake up and see that you are really something much more vast than even that special somebody. You are just living out this particular sequence, this dream sequence. And that's all that dies—the dream sequence. You as awareness don't die.

That's what's missing, for the most part, in death and dying literature. If you trace where we come from in our ideas about death and dying in this country, you'll see we began with a kind of fatalistic materialism: "Well, it's in the cards." Originally, there had been a religious tradition in this country which said that you go to heaven or you go to hell after death. Then along came more and more materialism, and with it came a sense that death is the "end." Thus, the intensive care unit, which keeps us alive at any cost, because who we are is our material identity. And so now we are transplanting organs and we are trying to get the body to last longer and longer.

Brother David Steindl-Rast

Brother David Steindl-Rast holds degrees from the Vienna Academy of the Fine Arts and the Psychological Institute and received his PhD in experimental psychology from the University of Vienna. He came to the United States with just a toothbrush and a copy of Martin Buber's *I and Thou* in his knapsack, then joined the newly founded Benedictine monastery of Mount Saviour in Elmira, New York, where he received training in philosophy and theology.[6]

Kramer: Brother David, let's begin with a creative question: What do you think is missing for most people with regard to their attitudes toward death and dying, the presence of which would transform their approach to death?

Br. David: I'll just tell you what comes to my mind off-hand. What's really missing is [being] fully alive. Because if we were fully alive right now, we wouldn't have to worry about being fully alive when it comes to dying and at that time we would know how to deal with it. You have to be very alive to deal with dying. It is something very active—the word "to die" in the English language, as in many other languages, has no passive voice. You can't say "I am being died." If you are "being died" you come out green or blue, but not dead. You can be killed and you will be killed sooner or later by something, but you have to die. That is something that you have to actively do. And so, if you really know how to live actively, you would also be able to die actively when life asks that from you.

If you were interviewing another person about your subject of interest, how would you begin the interview? Would you consider using the "what's missing" question? If not, how would you decide what question to begin with?

POINTS TO REMEMBER

Interview dialogues are a specific type of dialogue in which, after asking a knowledgeable person preplanned questions, one transitions into a spontaneous, unscripted exchange.

- It is most important to make the interviewee feel comfortable, feel important, and feel heard.
- Two essential elements of interview dialogues are discernment listening and interactive questioning.
- Intercultural dialogue can best be practiced using Leonard Swidler's guidelines: from being willing to learn dialogically to practicing self-critical honesty and empathy.
- The "What's missing?" question prompts the interviewee to respond outside of preplanned responses.

NOTES

1. Leonard Swidler, "Humankind from the Age of Monologue to the Age of Global Dialogue," *Journal of Ecumenical Studies* 47, no. 3 (Summer 2012): 471.

2. Originally, Leonard Swidler composed "Dialogue Decalogue," which was published in the *Journal of Ecumenical Studies* 20,no. 1 (Winter 1983). This "sound bite" version of the ten principles is found in the work of Julia Sheetz-Willard, Per Faaland, Rebecca Mays, and Angela Ili *Journal of Ecumenical Studies*

3. Sheetz-Willard, Faaland, Mays, and Ilić , "Interreligious Dialogue Reconsidered."

4. Some of Kübler-Ross's books include *On Death and Dying*; *Questions and Answers on Death and Dying*; *Death: The Final Stage of Growth*; and *To Live Until We Say Goodbye*. The complete interview can be found in "You Cannot Die Alone: Dr. Elizabeth Kübler-Ross Interviewed by Kenneth Kramer," *Omega: Journal of Death and Dying*, 50, no.2 (2004/2005).

5. Ram Dass's other books include *The Only Dance There Is*; *Grist For The Mill*; *Miracle of Love: Stories of Neem Karoli Baba*; *How Can I Help?*; *Compassion in Action: Setting Out on the Path of Service*; *Still Here: Embracing Aging, Changing and Dying*; *One-Liners: A Mini-Manual for a Spiritual Life*; and *Paths to God: Living the Bhagavad Gita*.

6. Some of his books include *Gratefulness: The Heart of Prayer*; *A Listening Heart: The Spirituality of Sacred Sensuousness*; *Common Sense Spirituality*; and *Deeper Than Words: Living the Apostles' Creed*. The complete interview can be found in "Dying Before Dying: Interview with Brother David Steindl-Rast," *Journal of Ecumenical Studies* 45, no. 4 (Fall 2010). It can also be accessed on YouTube by searching "Death and Spirituality."

Chapter Eight

Journal Dialogues

Have you ever asked yourself—or your students—if the methods you use to teach actually helped them learn? Have you ever reflected upon your teaching and wondered how it could be improved? Have you ever wished you could just talk it out with yourself? Or have you ever wondered how to continue learning from the materials taught year after year?

THE JOURNAL AS THOU

This chapter addresses several practices for generating fresh dialogue with yourself as well as with course ideas. While these methods are usually assigned to students, they are particularly appropriate for teachers. If journal work is to generate spontaneous discussions without pressure, discussion must flow freely from *both* sides.

In keeping with Buber's dialogical approach to human experience, how we use the journal is extremely important. Rather than an obligation that we perform in the spirit of grudging resistance, the journal becomes the embodiment of a living I-Thou relationship. We approach it as we would approach a person with whom we are in a deeply meaningful relationship, such as a close friend or partner.

Being in dialogue with course materials also puts one in dialogue with oneself. Being in dialogue with oneself allows one to reflect on the changing self, on how new ideas can become effective, on different answers that one might have given to the same questions at different times in life. Being in dialogue with others allows for reflection on how insights are reshaped when brought into relationship with another person. Being in dialogue through a journal allows one to practice this central relational art.

Each time that one writes, in a sense, the answer, the conversation, the exploration is actually writing itself! This becomes more natural as one becomes more adept at recording one's thoughts without evaluating, judging, embellishing, or adding anything that does not suggest itself. When the writing ends, it can be read back to oneself, and any considerations that finally suggest themselves can be added, but no editing should happen when one is writing spontaneously.

JOURNAL KEEPING

The reason for keeping a journal is simple: it provides one with new maps for understanding course material, with an opportunity to explore new paradigms. This act allows one to pause in the commotion of life to recollect, record, and then share insights, questions, and intentions with others. Entries, when made with an open mind and open heart, and when brought into genuine dialogue with others, provide invaluable openings into the material.

When we record insights that capture elusive feelings and experiences, it becomes easier to enter more authentically into the midst of the material studied. Every journal exercise is designed to lead journal keepers naturally and organically, directly and indirectly, into genuine engagement with the self, the text, and the entire class.

Writing in a journal interrupts one's routine patterns of behavior and habits of mind. New understandings unfold. In the process, we gain access to our unique inner resources and become more focused and disciplined in our outer engagements. Inwardly, the journal provides a means of reaching elusive and intuitive insights; outwardly, the journal reinforces the value of the educational process. The journal thus forms a bridge over which we cross back and forth between knowledge and understanding.

Every person brings his or her own understanding of the material studied into the journal process. This is essential to the use of journal keeping as a pedagogical tool. It is one place where we are not concerned with right or wrong, but with intellectual development through personal engagement. Rather than being concerned about the rightness of one understanding over another, we are concerned with getting multiple points of view to interact with each other.

THE DIALOGUE JOURNAL

A journal is not an end in itself, though we usually think of it as a private experience. Instead, it inspires a new dedication for entering into dialogue with an open mind and open heart. Journal keeping challenges teachers and students to rejuvenate their stand in the world. This provides teachers with a valuable opportunity to develop new ideas and reintegrate student responses into lecture.

There are several types of journals that can be beneficially used in an academic context. The dialogue journal, for instance, is an instrument for effectively recognizing the I-Thou nature of the relationships we have with others. It helps us to recognize correlations between outer and inner dialogues and then to apply and integrate these recognitions into our lives.

Ira Progoff captures the effect of journal writing on the human psyche when he writes that what this practice opens up is something far more than personal reflection: "This is the *elan vital* of our inner self. It is being re-awakened and re-energized, and given a personal frame of reference that will enable it to do its work and find its unique meaning for each of us in the context of our life history as we live it in the midst of the world."[1]

Dialogue journals enable users to draw upon outer and inner resources for personal growth and wholeness, but do this in a specifically I-Thou-centered way. Journal entries may contain one of three types of dialogue, or some combination of the three. These are outer dialogues, inner dialogues, and feedback dialogues.

OUTER, INNER, FEEDBACK

Outer dialogues record recalled words from actual, direct, honest, genuine, mutual exchanges taken from the writer's organic memory. In reconstructing these meaningful dialogues, try including a brief description of the person and the situation in which dialogue occurred, along with the words themselves as accurately as can be remembered and feelings about them at the time.

Inner dialogues record what happens when the writer listens in silence to his or her own central questions, needs, and concerns; in the silence of looking inward, letting images and insights take form as if from nowhere.

The point in this type of dialogue is to reflect on one's inner concerns. One should try not to impose ideas, but simply behold them. While listening, without thinking, remain open to whatever presents itself in the form of images, impressions, insights, recollections of a text, a person's words, actions or inactions that now emerge with new meaning.

Feedback dialogues record interactions with both the inner and the outer dialogues. How do they respond to each other? How does one answer what the other asks? How do they both complete and challenge each other? In other words, the writer pays attention to what unfolds between the inner and outer dialogues, the self and other. He or she attempts to *imagine the real* and then record the interaction between the real outside and the real inside, between the I and the Thou.

TURNING POINTS

Indeed, a major purpose of keeping a Dialogue Journal is to practice I-Thou reflections, which gives journal keepers an effective personal perspective. After recording several outer and inner dialogues, reread with these questions. Consider asking: (1) How do my inner and outer dialogues speak to each other? and, most importantly, (2) How and where can the correlation between them be integrated into my life?

The momentum that builds from outer, inner, and feedback dialogues results in *turning points* that can radically expand and reshape one's views.

Journals are a forum in which one can achieve "break-through" insights into the course material. Buber used the word "break-through" in its hyphenated form rather than as a compound single word to emphasize its active element—breaking through.

Rather than an exalted, heroic, once-and-for-all life change, a turning point implies breaking through again and again from one's dully tempered, habitual routines into dialogical responsibility for our everyday realities. Journal prompts that emerge from the heart of each topic, therefore, are aimed at moving one from monologue to dialogue with topic at hand.

JOURNAL GUIDELINES

The purpose of a journal is to offer teachers and students alike a method for understanding course materials and for discovering interpersonal growth. In this sense, the journal records a double dialogue—an opportunity for journal keepers to express inner world views and attitudes as well as to express their relationships to the material, be they critical, sympathetic, or disinterested. In either instance, opportunity for a deeper understanding and a better integration of the materials is afforded. The following guidelines can be used as a framework for journal writing.

1. Let your journal be a "Thou," a friend, and allow your writing in it to be an enjoyable, perhaps cathartic, experience.
2. Date each entry so you may track the progression of your opinions, feelings, and beliefs.
3. The first entry in the journal should include your course goals, what you expect to receive from this course.
4. Entries include responses to the readings and especially to what happens in the classroom along with subsequent reactions.
5. At times, reflect upon previously expressed positions and presuppositions through which you have been viewing the materials. Record new points of view. For example, you may wish to record mistaken ideas

you have held and what you have learned from these misunderstandings.

6. The last entry in the journal can be a critical reflection on the journal process itself, in which you evaluate your own self-discoveries as a result of the journal process.

As should be apparent, the journal is an open forum, a portable laboratory meant to encourage each writer's own inventiveness.

CRITICAL AND IMAGINATIVE RESPONSES

Typically, dialogue journals have two orientations. The first orientation, critical thinking, refers to a cognitive analysis of questions, topics, and issues that arise from the reading, class discussions, and contemporary media. The second orientation, imaginative experiments, encourages students to write imaginative responses to the class materials.

Critical thinking exercises are designed to provoke analysis of the course data. These hone the skills of argument, expansion, and comparison. The aim of critical thinking questions is to learn to teach ourselves through re-expression of the material and to learn by noting our mistakes. The purpose of these exercises is to make personal the human experiences of the texts. Through comparisons, we are drawn more deeply into the material.

Imaginative experiments are designed to encourage intuitive thinking and more inventive responses to the material. Whereas the critical thinking aspect of journal writing is more rational, the imaginative aspect is more tacit. It includes dialogues, reveries, role-switching activities, and rewriting passages from a text in one's own words.

A teacher's imagining new ways to present old materials and a student's presenting new ideas combine to enable each to connect more deeply to the material and to each other. Each journalist, depending on the quality of one's journal, grows as a teacher, as a student, and as a person.

ACADEMIC JOURNAL

Another variety of journal work has been called by Maurice Friedman the "academic journal." An academic journal is a qualitative research tool with four reciprocal elements:

1. Quote a personally significant passage from the reading or class discussion.
2. Rewrite it in your own words, not paraphrasing, but imagining the other person's viewpoint.

3. Respond to it from where you stand; enter into dialogue with it at any level, intellectually and/or emotionally.
4. Apply your dialogue to a recurring issue in the course, or in your life.[2]

After completing these four steps, teachers and students can share what they have written or comment on the exercise itself. Again, it is helpful to stress that the dialogue is refreshed and refreshing when teachers can share with students as well as vice versa.

The point is not to arrive at one right view; rather, it is to prompt responses to reflections that have been shared by others. In the process, class materials are clarified, individual dialogues are cross-fertilized, and personal stories are introduced that enrich and deepen the dialogical context. As a young woman excitedly remarked after a Psychology and Religious Experience class, "I look forward to reading my journal entries because then I can hear what others think about what I think."

DIALOGUE SCRIPTS

A variation on this approach is the dialogue script, in which one is invited to create dialogues between yourself and another person, such as the author of a text. "Underlying these written dialogues," writes Ira Progoff, "is the more fundamental sense of dialogue not as a technique but as a way of relationship."[3] One can create dialogue scripts with works, the body, events, dreams, society, and one's inner wisdom. Based on an adaptation of Progoff's instructions to write without "censorship or conscious direction," one might go about this by:

- sitting in quietness;
- imagining the other person by placing yourself inside the actuality of their life as though participating in it;
- rehearsing concrete details of what you know about the life and thought of the person;
- addressing a question about the material that we have studied to this imagined other;
- then, feeling the presence of the other, with eyes closed, listening to what the other might say without deliberately thinking about it, write in your journal.

Dialogue scripts offer a unique way to creatively develop and synthesize information, and a way to seek the common ground of dialogue between disparate ideas. They also develop the ability to draw intelligent inferences from observations and reinforce the critical and knowledge-based goals of the class. "It may be that when we read the dialogue script to ourselves a further dialogue is immediately stimulated," especially, it can be added, with others both in and out of class.[4]

ASK YOURSELF

If journal keeping offers journalists opportunities for deep reflection on the educational process, it is worth asking oneself three questions: What am I doing in the classroom? Why am I doing it? How can it be done in the best possible way?

How would you design a journal exercise that would, in turn, challenge a person to expand intellectual/emotive boundaries that at times encase us? Would it be better to arrive at a single answer that integrates each of these separate questions? Or to address these questions separately?

What just happened? To the extent that you engaged or were engaged by these questions, you shifted your stance from one-sided, I-It relation to two-sided, I-Thou relationship. While journal exercises begin in the I-It mode, they offer an opening for an I-Thou engagement, for the emergence of new perspectives, new questions.

POINTS TO REMEMBER

Journal dialogues—with others, with texts, with art, with the class—provide occasions for deep reflection on the course and on how it can be integrated.

- The purpose of keeping a journal is to clarify the journal keeper's views, which provide further opportunity to dialogue with others.
- The journal, for a teacher, allows him or her to make fresh connections with the course material and rediscover his or her students.
- The journal forms a bridge over which we cross back and forth between knowledge and understanding.
- Three forms of journal keeping are outer dialogues, inner dialogues, and feedback dialogues.
- Journaling addresses three important educative questions: What am I doing? Why am I doing it? How can it be done better?

NOTES

1. Ira Progoff, *At a Journal Workshop* (New York: Dialogue House Library, 1975), 45.
2. Maurice Friedman, *The Confirmation of Otherness, in Family, Community, and Society* (New York: Pilgrim Press, 1983), 157.

3. Progoff, *At a Journal Workshop*, 159.
4. Progoff, *At a Journal Workshop*, 268.

Conclusion

Referring to his remark that "relationship educates," Buber was once asked how is it possible to liberate the relationship of the individual . . . to her- or himself? In response, Buber chose to speak of the educator's first task. That task, he said, must "again and again be decided, according to the individual and the situation." How? Only by guiding students in a pedagogical manner that is "unemotional, unromantic, unsentimental . . . toward coming into a genuine contact with the reality accessible to him [and her].

But, you say, he lacks the courage. How does one educate for courage? Through nourishing trust. How does one nourish trust? Through one's own trustworthiness."[1]

To be relevant, "education must not only provide for the reproduction of skills, but also for their progress."[2] It follows, for this reason, that knowledge is best transmitted, understood, and applied in response to all educative voices. Buber's dialogical principles allow us not only to receive data but to arrange it in new ways, by connecting together and responding to all voices.

Learning through dialogue, its theory and methods, its application and practices, can be discussed indefinitely since its meaning is not fixed. A dialogical teacher creates openness for encounter to take place between the one who pursues learning and the one who assists in the educational process. Each educational situation is unique.

FINDINGS

How did Buber respond to the classical and progressive educational practices of his day? Unable to accept either objectivist teacher-directed or subjectivist student-generated approaches, Martin Buber opened up a third way—his intersubjective approach, which embodies reciprocal interactions between and among teacher, student, and teaching.

In these chapters, we encountered the significance of Buber's educational theory, I-Thou dialogical knowing and I-It individual knowledge. As well, we considered his method of inclusion, which embodies listening to another person empathetically to experience the other's side of the conversation.

We learned that teaching becomes unteaching when one is able to let go of being one hundred percent in control of the class and allows oneself to be directed by the dynamic rhythm of intersubjectivity. We also found that dialogue becomes a meta-methodology when its practice—turning, listening, addressing, and responding—facilitates the integration and challenge of contrasting, even conflicting views.

We saw how dialogue with texts occurs only to the extent that the text is engaged as a Thou, as a voice that invites response. And we saw that dialogues with students, when reciprocal, are a force that energizes the address-response educational process.

We were then able to practice Buber's theory/method in two different yet similar dialogical expressions. Interview dialogues provide an opportunity for the interviewer to transition from asking preplanned questions into an unscripted exchange. Journal dialogues—with other, with texts, with art, and with the class—provide occasions for deep reflection on what you are doing, why you are doing it, and how it can best be done.

Through dialogue, both teacher and students observe and critically analyze course content, together contributing to an interpersonal, reciprocal educative process. Although a dialogical pedagogy cannot be summarized, it can be characterized by six key elements. Choosing a dialogical stance in the classroom describes one who practices:

1. *Relationship*—Real knowing happens in the midst of a multi-sided relationship, which is present, open, dialogical, and has potential for a future.
2. *Inclusivity*—Inclusion, or imagining what another is thinking, feeling, and experiencing, is the irreplaceable method for learning dialogically.
3. *Reciprocity*—Neither objective, nor subjective, intersubjective learning happens mutually between persons and content.
4. *Openness*—Educating dialogically results in presence, directness, and responsibility.
5. *Personalizing*—Dialogue with texts, art, nature, ideas, feelings, things requires encountering the other personally.
6. *Trusting*—The educative potency of intersubjective dialogues between/among teacher, students, and material.

The value of a dialogical pedagogy lies in its awakening of the instructor's educated voice, the students' learning voices, and the dialogical teaching voice and lies in its ability to recover interhuman relationships. In turning toward the other, addressing his or her presence, listening empathically, and responding responsibly, one's character is refined, one's convictions are shaped and reshaped.

WHAT'S NEXT?

Our summarizing discussion of how Buber's dialogical principles transform teaching and learning is an appropriate place to conclude because of what it implies, but doesn't say outright. That is: the best place to understand Buber's thought is not in classrooms or the scholar's study, but in everyday life-encounters between people.

We are in this together. By assisting students to become dialogical—and yourself in the process—we learn not only how to be present, but also how to experience the other's side. We mutually recognize the transformative value of overcoming one-sided solitude. Mutual dialogues are in themselves educative.

What we realize is a break-through: the opening of a direct relationship with learning. Teacher and students learn to respond responsibly to each new situation. Our particular uniqueness transforms in the engagement. Small wonder that this book ends by elaborating upon where it began—the reciprocal nature of genuine dialogue educates.

NOTES

1. Martin Buber, *Philosophical Interrogations,* ed. Sydney and Beatrice Rome (New York: Holt, Rinehart, 1964), 63.
2. Jean-Francois Lyotard, *The Postmodern Condition: A Report on Knowledge* (Minneapolis: University of Minnesota Press, 1993), 52.

Critical Terms

Addressing: *Anrede* refers to accepting and affirming the unique presence of the other, to asking meaningful questions, and to listening attentively to the response.

Being: *Wesen* refers not to an abstract concept from which other concepts can be derived, but to the whole living reality of a thing that manifests in relationship to other things. A solitary single one has no meaning.

Between: *Zwischen* refers to the immediate presence of unreserved, spontaneous mutuality common to each partner, yet beyond the sphere of either, which happens on the "narrow ridge" between either/or, between competing absolutes, where we become wholly and uniquely human. Impossible to objectify, "the between" is the most true reality of human existence. The between is thus not something that is fixed but always becomes in the dynamic of relationship.

Confirmation: *Bestätigung* is the act of continuing to take a dialogical stand in the presence of the other, affirming, accepting, and supporting the other in her/his uniqueness, even if opposing the other when necessary.

Dialogue: *Dialog, das Gespräch* refers to open, direct, mutual, communication (spoken or silent) between persons who turn wholly toward the other, speak spontaneously without withholding or promoting an agenda, listen attentively, and respond responsibly. It cannot take place when one thinks or speaks monologically but only in an actual encounter with a living other. Genuine dialogue cannot be demanded or planned.

Education: *Erziehung, Bildung* refers not to instruction in a skill, a trade, or a profession, but to a calling forth and a development of a student's character. To ask of the educator is to ask of the student the desire to assume his or her responsibility to respond openly and honestly in each unique situation to whatever is encountered.

Encounter: *Begegnung* refers to an unanticipated interaction or direct communication between our innermost being and who/what presents itself to us. The word *Begegnung* signifies a sudden, unplanned occurrence of engaging and being engaged. Each encounter is unique, never occurs in the same form, even though it occurs between the same persons.

Event: *Das Ereignis* occurs when a person enters into a unique encounter with the other and thus develops an ever-renewed connection with the other. Rather than a one-sided experience, in which an individual maintains his or her position regardless of what the other says, feels, or thinks, an event is always two-sided.

Experience: *Erfahrung* refers to perceiving the phenomenal world in an *I-It* manner through sensations and concepts in order to use, analyze, or classify. In this domain, one experiences external attributes of the other.

Erlebnis refers to an inner experience which, no matter how powerful, remains one-sided in contradiction to genuine *I-Thou* relationship, in which there is an immediate living encounter with a unique other, as subject with subject.

I: *Ich* refers to either the individual I, who expresses his or her relation to the world as an It, or to the relational I, who expresses his or her relationship to the world as a Thou. The I, taken by itself, without relation to an It, or without relationship to a Thou, is only an abstraction that may be analyzed, studied, described, but not encountered as a living being.

Inclusion: *Umfassung* refers to "making present," imagining what the other person is thinking, feeling, and experiencing (not as detached content but as a living process) without surrendering one's own stand. In the teacher-student relationship, for Buber, inclusion is one-sided in that the student is not yet ready or able to practice experiencing the teacher's side of the relationship.

Individual: *Eigenwesen* refers to people who put their needs into the center of their actions and stand to the world in an *I-It* relation. One is an individual in the sense of being a singular I who responds to whomever or whatever is encountered in a one-sided manner. The individual, however, is neither the starting point nor the goal of existence.

Interhuman: *Das Zwischenmenschliche* refers to the interactive region that happens between persons participating in genuine relationship, to the spirit of "the between" through which a person becomes whole and can glimpse the ultimate source of life.

Intersubjective: *Intersubjektiv* refers to the self and voice, the speaking and listening, the perspectives and experiences of each person or subject in relationship who remains open to learning and changing through each real dialogical encounter. The term can also be used, when speaking about the study of "religion," in place of the word interhuman.

It: *Es* refers to relating to the world as an object of observation, classification, or conceptualization. The It, therefore, finally is an abstraction from living experience. "It" may be either a single fact of observation or a complete worldview, even a field theory of the universe.

Knowing: *Wissen* refers to an intellectual and emotional connection with person, texts, or ideas in which one comprehends what one is connected to.

Listening: *Zuhoeren* refers to turning with obedient attention to the signs of address; to imagining what the other is thinking, feeling, and experiencing; to discerning what is said and what is not said.

Monologue: *Der Monologue* refers to that situation in which two or more people speak at each other in circuitous ways and yet imagine they have escaped the separation of being thrown back on their own resources.

Mutuality: *Gegenseitigkeit* refers to the full, spontaneous, and reciprocal participation of each partner in genuine relationship.

Object: *Gegenstand* refers to an *I-It* relation to the other, viewing or relating to the other as a thing to be observed, measured, and classified. In this process, one's knowing is distanced or separated from the other, as distinguished from the immediate subject-subject, relational, I-Thou knowing. Objective reality is thus regarded as outside of the human subject.

Pedagogy: *Pädagogik* refers to ways that educational theory and method are applied and practiced in teaching, whether as an academic subject or other types of information.

Person: *Person* refers to one who wholly enters into relationship with a *Thou*, accepting the other as an equal partner while yet taking a personal stand. Buber consistently maintains a contrast between "person" and "individual" (*Eigenwesen*). The person lives *with* the world; an individual lives *in* the world. The person becomes conscious of him- or herself as co-existent and, thus, as a whole human being, whereas the individual knows him- or herself only in isolation.

Present/Presence: *Gegenwart* can mean in German either "present" or "presence." Therefore, "presence" has a double dynamic: (1) being fully "there" without withholding oneself; and (2) being fully "open" to enter into ever-renewed dialogue with others. Present, thus, is not a temporal concept of frozen time, but rather being fully there at the moment of engagement.

Reality: *Wirklichkeit* refers not to something given that may be described or explained in objective terms but to something that occurs in acts of relationship. Reality is not in the I or the It, nor in the Thou, but only between I and Thou. One knows reality only by participating in its occurrence in relationship.

Reflexion: *Rueckbiegung* refers to a monological turning away from others and toward self-preoccupations. Literally, the self curves back on itself, eliminating the possibility of dialogue.

Relationship: *Beziehung* refers to a mutual presence, to *I-Thou* relationships that embody a past, a present, and a potential for the future. Relationship refers to a close human bonding in which both partners affirm, accept, and confirm each other.

Responding: *Antworten* refers to replying openly and honestly to the unique sights, signs, and words that continuously address us, without judging, dismissing, or withdrawing.

Responsibility: *Verantwortung* refers to being answerable for your words and actions in life. Genuine responsibility, for Buber, exists only where there is honest, open, and direct responding to who or what is encountered.

Speaking: *Gespräch* refers to an open-ended conversation with another that happens on an equal basis between persons without agendas.

Stand: *Haltung* refers to one's position, stance, or bearing in the world in the presence of a dialogical partner or nature or spirit becoming forms. It is through this "bearing" toward an other (either *I-It* or *I-Thou*) that one communicates and thereby comes into existence.

Thou: *Das Du* refers to the other who or that is encountered by a person in the *I-Thou* relationship. As its own whole and unique being, the Thou exists independently of the I, yet has meaning only in their interaction. The term Thou refers to being encountered, addressed, and responded to by the I. As a whole and unique being, the Thou may also become an I when it addresses the other as its Thou. The Thou is always unique, always new, since no encounter between an I and a Thou repeats itself in the same way.

Turning: *Umkehr* refers to an inner transformation that opens one to enter wholeheartedly in the presence of the other, without holding back. Turning embodies a double movement: *from* separation, and *toward* deep bonding.

Works Cited

Bakhtin, Mikhail. *Speech Genres and Other Late Essays*, trans. Vern McGee. Austin: University of Texas Press, 1986.

Beckett, Samuel. *Waiting for Godot*. New York: Grove Press, 1954.

Buber, Martin. "Advice to Frequenters of Libraries," Books for Your Vacation. *Branch Library Book News* (The New York Public Library) 21, no. 5 (1944).

———. *A Believing Humanism*, trans. Maurice Friedman. New York: Simon and Schuster, 1969.

———. *Between Man and Man*, trans. Ronald Gregor Smith. New York: The Macmillan Company, 1948.

———. *Between Man and Man*, with introduction and afterword: "The History of the Dialogical Principle," trans. Ronald Gregor Smith, Maurice Friedman. New York: Collier Books, 1965.

———. *I and Thou*, trans. Ronald Gregor Smith, 2nd edition. New York: Charles Scribner's Sons, 1937/1958.

———. *I and Thou*, trans. Walter Kaufmann. New York: Charles Scribner's Sons, 1970.

———. *Israel and the World, Essays in a Time of Crisis*. New York: Schocken Books, 1948.

———. *The Knowledge of Man*, trans. with introduction by Maurice Friedman. New York: Harper & Row, 1965.

———. *Mamre: Essays in Religion*, trans. Greta Hort. Westport, Conn.: Greenwood Press, 1946.

———. *Meetings*, ed. Maurice Friedman. Chicago: Open Court, 1973.

———. "A New Venture in Adult Education." *The Hebrew University of Jerusalem*, Semi-Jubilee Volume (Jerusalem: The Hebrew University, April 1950), 117.

———. *On Judaism*, ed. Nahum N. Glatzer. New York: Schocken Books, 1972.

———. *Philosophical Interrogations*, ed. Sydney and Beatrice Rome. New York: Holt, Rinehart, 1964.

———. *The Philosophy of Martin Buber*, ed. Paul Arthur Schilpp and Maurice Friedman. La Salle, Ill.: Open Court, 1967.

———. *Pointing the Way*, trans. Maurice Friedman. New York: Schocken Books, 1957.

———. *Tales of the Hasidim: Early Masters*, trans. Olga Marx. New York: Shocken Books, 1991.

———. *Tales of the Hasidim: The Later Masters*, trans. Olga Marx. New York: Schocken Books, 1948.

Cain, Susan. *Quiet: the Power of Introvert in a World That Can't Stop Talking*. New York: Crown Publishing, 2012.

Cox, Harvey. *The Secular City*. New York: The Macmillan Company, 1965.

Credaro, A. B. "Research Findings: The Relationship between School Libraries and Academic Achievement." *Principal Matters* 53 (November 2002): 35–36.

DeMillo, Richard. *Abelard to Apple: The Fate of American Colleges and Universities*. Massachusetts: MIT Press, 2011.

———. "The Future Can't Wait." *New York Times*, November 6, 2011.

Durkheim, Emile. *Elementary Forms of the Religious Life*. New York: Macmillan, 1915.

Eck, Diana. *Encountering God: A Spiritual Journey from Bozeman to Banaras*. Boston: Beacon Press, 1993.

Evans-Pritchard, E. E. *Theories of Primitive Religion*. New York: Oxford University Press, 1968.

Fader, Larry. *120'00": A Conversation with John Cage*. Maine: Nine Point Publishing, 2012.

Foster, Thomas C. *How to Read Literature like a Professor*. New York: Harper, 2003.

Friedman, Maurice. *The Confirmation of Otherness, in Family, Community, and Society*. New York: Pilgrim Press, 1983.

———. *A Dialogue with Hasidic Tales: Hallowing the Everyday*. New York: Insight Books, 1988.

———. *Encounter on the Narrow Ridge: A Life of Martin Buber*. New York: Paragon House, 1991.

———, ed. *Martin Buber and the Human Sciences*. New York: State University of New York Press, 1996.

———. *Martin Buber: The Life of Dialogue*. Chicago: The University of Chicago Press, 1955.

———. "Martin Buber and Mikhail Bakhtin: The Dialogue of Voices and the Word That Is Spoken." *Religion and Literature* 33 (2001).

———. *My Friendship with Martin Buber*. New York: Syracuse University Press, 2013.

———. *Religion and Psychology: A Dialogical Approach*. New York: Paragon House, 1992.

———. *Touchstones of Reality: Existential Trust and the Community of Peace*. New York: E. P. Dutton, 1972.

Friedman, Maurice, in association with David Damico. *Genuine Dialogue and Real Partnership: Foundations of True Community*. Bloomington, Ind.: Trafford Publishing, 2011.

———. *My Friendship with Martin Buber*. New York: Syracuse University Press, 2013.

Goes, Albrecht. *Men of Dialogue: Martin Buber and Albrecht Goes*, ed. William Rollins and Harry Zohn. New York: Funk & Wagnalls, 1969.

Guilar, Joshua D. "Intersubjectivity and Dialogic instruction." *Radical Pedagogy* 8, no. 1 (2006). Retrieved Dec. 21, 2011, from radicalpedagogy.icaap.org/content/issue8_1.

Helfand, David J. "Where Tradition Goes to the Back of the Class." *The New York Times*, January 22, 2012.

Hendley, Brian. "Martin Buber on the Teacher/Student Relationship: A Critical Appraisal." *Journal of Philosophy of Education* 12 (1978): 143. (Hendley's reference to Dewey is taken from John Dewey, *Democracy and Education* [New York: Macmillan, 1916].)

Hermida, Julian. "The Importance of Teaching Academic Reading Skills in First-Year University Courses." *The International Journal of Research and Review* 3 (September 2009).

Hodes, Aubrey. *Martin Buber: An Intimate Portrait*. New York: Viking Press, 1971.

Hunt, Russell A. "Reading and Writing for Real: Why It Matters for Learning." *Atlantic Universities' Teaching Showcase* 55.

Hycner, Richard. *Between Person and Person: Toward a Dialogical Psychotherapy*. New York: The Gestalt Press, 1991.

James, William. *The Varieties of Religious Experience*. New York: Longmans, Green & Co., 1902.

Kepnes, Stephen. *The Text as Thou: Martin Buber's Dialogical Hermeneutics and Narrative Theology*. Bloomington: Indiana University Press, 1992.

Kramer, Kenneth. "Cross-Reanimating Martin Buber's 'Between' and Shin'ichi Hisamatsu's 'Nothingness.'" *Journal of Ecumenical Studies* 46, no. 3 (Summer 2011).

———, ed. *Dialogically Speaking: Maurice Friedman's Interdisciplinary Humanism*. Eugene, Ore.: Pickwick Publications, 2011.

———. "Dying Before Dying: Interview with Brother David Steindl-Rast." *Journal of Ecumenical Studies* 45, no. 4 (Fall 2010).

———. *Martin Buber's* I and Thou, *Practicing Living Dialogue*. New York: Paulist Press, 2003.

———. *The Sacred Art of Dying : How World Religions Understand Death*. New York: Paulist Press, 1988.

———. "Through Each Other's Eyes: A Shin Buddhist-Catholic Dialogue." *The Pacific World New Series*, no. 8 (Fall 1992): 84–92.

———. "Unteaching Religious Studies." *The Council on the Study of Religion Bulletin* 15, no. 4 (October 1984).

———. *World Scriptures: An Introduction to Comparative Religions*. New York: Paulist Press, 1986.

———. "You Cannot Die Alone: Doctor Elisabeth Kübler-Ross Interviewed by Kenneth Kramer." *Omega: Journal of Death and Dying* 50, no. 2 (2004/2005).

Krapanzano, Vincent. "On Dialogue," in *The Interpretation of Dialogue*, ed. by Tullio Maranhao. Chicago: University of Chicago Press, 1990.

Lyotard, Jean-Francois. *The Postmodern Condition: A Report on Knowledge*. Minneapolis: University of Minnesota Press, 1993.

Moody, A. David. *Thomas Stearns Eliot: Poet*. Cambridge: Cambridge University Press, 1979.

Otto, Rudolf. *The Idea of the Holy*. New York: Oxford University Press, 1958.

Paden, William E. *Interpreting the Sacred: Ways of Viewing Religion*. Boston: Beacon Press, 1992/2003.

Palmer, Parker J. *The Courage to Teach: Exploring the Inner Landscape of a Teacher's Life*. San Francisco: Jossey-Bass, 1997.

———. *Reflections* 99, no. 1 (Spring 2012).

Pound, Ezra. *ABC of Reading*. New York: New Directions, 1960.

Progoff, Ira. *At a Journal Workshop*. New York: Dialogue House Library, 1975.

Sampson, Edward. *Celebrating the Other: A Dialogic Account of Human Nature*. Boulder, Colo.: Westview, 1993.

Scott, Charles. *Becoming Dialogue; Martin Buber's Concept of Turning to the Other as Educational Praxis*. PhD diss., Simon Fraser University, 2011.

Sheetz-Willard, Julia, Per Faaland, Rebecca Mays, and Angela Ilić. "Interreligious Dialogue Reconsidered: Learning from and Responding to Critique and Change." *Journal of Ecumenical Studies* 47, no. 2 (Spring 2012).

Silverman, Gillian. "It's Alive!" *New York Times Book Review*, August 12, 2012.

Simon, Ernst. "Martin Buber, The Educator," in *The Philosophy of Martin Buber*, ed. Paul Arthur Schilpp and Maurice Friedman. LaSalle, Ill.: Open Court, 1967.

———. to Martin Buber, November 2, 1923, in *The Letters of Martin Buber*, ed. Nahum M. Glatzer and Paul Mendes-Flohr. New York: Syracuse University Press, 1991.

Smith, Wilfred Cantwell. "Comparative Religion: Whither and Why?" in *The History of Religions: Essays in Methodology*, ed. Mircea Eliade and Joseph M. Kitagawa. Chicago: University of Chicago Press, 1959.

———. *The Meaning and End of Religion*. New York: Fortress Press, 1962.

Swidler, Leonard. "Dialogue Decalogue." *Journal of Ecumenical Studies* 20, no. 1 (Winter 1983).

———. "Humankind from the Age of Monologue to the Age of Global Dialogue." *Journal of Ecumenical Studies* 47, no. 3 (Summer 2012).

Tillich, Paul. "Personal Introduction to My Systematic Theology." *Modern Theology* 1, no. 2 (January 1985).

Traina, Richard. "What Makes a Good Teacher." *Education Week*, January 20, 1999.

Tubbs, Nigel. *Philosophy of the Teacher*. Oxford: Blackwell Publishing, 2005.

Turkle, Sherry. *Alone Together: Why We Expect More from Technology and Less from Each Other*. New York: Basic Books, 2011.

———. "The Flight from Conversation." Sunday Review, *New York Times*, April 22, 2011.

Tweed, Thomas A. *Crossing and Dwelling: A Theory of Religion*. Cambridge, Mass: Harvard University Press, 2008.

Waardenburg, Jacques, ed. *Classical Approaches to the Study of Religion*. Berlin: de Gruyter, 1999.

Waley, Arthur, trans. *The Analects of Confucius*. New York: Vintage Books, 1938.
Weinstein, Joshua. *Buber and Humanistic Education*. New York: Philosophical Library, 1975.
Whitehead, Alfred North. *Religion in the Making*. New York: New American Library, 1926.
Yaron, Kalmon. "Martin Buber." *Prospects: The Quarterly Review of Comparative Education* 23, no. 1/2 (1993): 135–46.

Index

About the Author

Kenneth Paul Kramer is professor emeritus of comparative religious studies at San José (California) State University where he taught from 1976 to 2001. He holds a BA from Temple University, a BD from Andover Newton Theological School, an STM from Yale Divinity School, and a PhD (1971) in religion and culture from Temple University. He has published *Martin Buber's Spirituality: Hasidic Wisdom for Everyday Life* (Rowman & Littlefield Publications, 2012); *Redeeming Time: T. S. Eliot's* Four Quartets (Cowley/Rowman & Littlefield Publications, 2007); *Martin Buber's* I and Thou*: Practicing Living Dialogue* (2003); *Death Dreams: Unveiling Mysteries of the Unconscious Mind* (1993); *The Sacred Art of Dying: How World Religions Understand Death* (1988); and *World Scriptures: An Introduction to Comparative Religions* (1986). He is also the editor of *Dialogically Speaking: Maurice Friedman's Interdisciplinary Humanism* (2011).